Dedication

To my husband John, who has always supported my ideas, including helping create Parent Booster USA to support parents and schools "keep legal" when managing their fundraising groups. And for supporting my baking habit by buying me a Kitchen Aid mixer years ago.

School Fundraising

School Fundraising

So Much More Than Cookie Dough

Sandra Pfau Englund, Esq.

School Fundraising: So Much More Than Cookie Dough

Copyright © 2015 by Sandra Pfau Englund.

All Rights Reserved. No part of this book may be reproduced, transmitted, or stored in any form or by any means whatsoever without express written permission in advance from the author, except in brief quotations in critical articles or reviews.

First printing 2015
ISBN: 978-0-9970878-0-2 (printed version)
ISBN: 978-0-9970878-1-9 (mobi and epub versions)

Cover and interior design by Adina Cucicov, Flamingo Designs.

Disclaimer

This book provides information and resources to help volunteers and schools manage parent teacher organizations, booster clubs, and other fundraising groups. This book does not provide legal or other professional advice. Please contact an appropriate professional if you need help with a specific issue relating to a school fundraising organization.

Use of information provided in this book is voluntary and should be used based on your own analysis of its accuracy and appropriateness for your intended use.

While effort was made to ensure the accuracy of the book's content at the time of publication, the information, rules and laws may have changed, or errors or omissions may occur.

Reference to specific commercial businesses, products, or services by trade name, trademark, manufacturer or otherwise in this book are for informational purposes only and does not imply the endorsement, recommendation, or favoring by the author or Parent Booster USA.

Foreword

If you are reading this book, chances are you are a good-hearted parent who's been asked to take on a big responsibility—to help a school fundraising organization. Or you may be a school principal, business officer or other school staff member whose been asked to add school fundraising group oversight to your already-too-full-plate of duties.

As a parent volunteer, you probably are focused on how you can raise enough funds to support your child's band, or sports team, or robotics club. You're excited and full of ideas. You likely never considered a school booster club as a business that was subject to federal and state tax and fundraising regulations. And who knew that you needed to worry about angry parents suing if a child gets injured at the fall festival, what is and is not deductible when someone buys the week at the beach at the silent auction, or having the funds you worked so hard to raise stolen by the booster club treasurer that you have known for years.

As a school administrator, you probably are worried about how to make sure multiple booster clubs don't try to sell cookie dough during the same month, or the limits of your authority to make sure your school doesn't end up in the headlines because the booster clubs have not filed their taxes, registered with the state before conducting BINGO or the 50/50 raffle, or allowed a volunteer to pocket the cash intended to support the school.

No worries. Sandra Pfau Englund throws you a life ring to help keep you and your school out of hot water. She makes sense of all the rules, provides checklists, tips and "recipes for success" so you can focus on what's important—the students and their activities. Read it, share it with your fellow volunteers and school staff that advise these groups,, and adopt the practices and procedures that will make you and your group look like you can walk on water.

How to Use This Book

This book is intended to be a fun and quick to read that provides a wealth of resources for managing a school fundraising group. Look for the paperclips throughout the book that mark the bonus materials—templates, checklists and guidelines—found in the appendices to the book and in electronic form on the companion website, **morecookiedough.com**. The tips and best practices I've learned in my 20+ years working with nonprofit groups are highlighted throughout the book as "Recipes for Success." And I've provided 10-second takeaway at the end of each chapter to provide a short summary of the key points (or provide an even quicker read for those of you with little time on your hands!)

About the Author

Shortly after moving to Northeastern North Carolina in the summer of 2003, I was asked to serve as the president of the PTO at my children's elementary school. Perhaps in a momentary error of judgment, I agreed. Little did I know what I had gotten myself into.

Our elementary school PTO was not incorporated, had no federal or state tax exempt status, never filed a tax return, and operated with no rules or financial controls. I also soon learned that balancing the interests of the parent volunteers, and the school and its staff, can be tricky. I was lucky, however. As a lawyer with a law firm that focuses on nonprofit start-ups, I knew how to get Grandy Primary PTO back in good shape. I realized then, however, that managing a school fundraising group was a daunting task requiring a wide range of skills to handle government regulation, accounting, marketing, fundraising, and lots of people skills.

It was during my tenure as the elementary school PTO president that I realized parents and schools need help navigating the complex and murky waterways of managing school fundraising groups. And so, Parent Booster USA was born—the only national nonprofit 501(c)(3) tax-exempt organization to provide the continuity and support needed by school fundraising groups. This book pulls together my 20+ years of experience working with school fundraising groups as a lawyer and as a mom.

In the News

"PBUSA cautions against the use of 'individual fundraising accounts'"—"Parent Booster Clubs—Raising Money for Your Own Kid is Not Charity,"
Forbes, Sept. 5, 2013

"A U.S. Tax Court ruling last month could snarl the tax-exempt status of thousands of booster clubs and similar groups across the country... Sandra Englund sees three courses of action..." "Booster Clubs Attract Scrutiny,"
Wall Street Journal, Sept. 13, 2013

"How can you make sure your child's booster club is protected from theft? Sandra Englund of Parent Booster USA ... recommends,"
Today on NBC, Jun. 3, 2014

Parent Booster USA and its executive director Sandra Pfau Englund are happy to serve as a one-stop resource on school fundraising organizations.

For information, or to book an appearance:
call 866-936-6209, or
email: **sandy@parentbooster.org**

Contents

PART I. THAT'S A LOT OF COOKIE DOUGH! 1

1 Selling cookie dough is complicated 3
A few notes about the tangled web of rules and laws that surround the school fundraising "business" without getting into trouble.

2 Selling cookie dough is important 5
Take a quick minute to pat yourself on the back. What you are doing to support education is important.

PART II. ASSEMBLE YOUR INGREDIENTS 9

3 Structure your group for more success and less risk 11
The ingredients and a checklist for setting up a school fundraising group.

4 Learn the rules of the game 17
A brief look at who regulates school fundraising

5 Even school fundraising groups have to file taxes 25
The IRS wants to jump into the mix when money is involved.

6 Your state wants a bite, too! 39
An outline of what your state government expects to know abut your school fundraising group

7 Tools & tidbits to make things easier 47
Notes, tips, and templates to help you handle your money, run your meetings, and limit your risks.

PART III. MORE FOOD FOR THOUGHT 69

8 Fundraising do's and don'ts 71
Deductions rules, donations receipts, and raffle rules all in one place

9 Blending school staff and volunteers 91
School staff and volunteers don't always make the best sandwich cookie. Learn how to stick the two together for success.

10 Adding in school fees 101
A few notes about boosters and school fees

11 Don't get burned by Title IX 105
Why even boosters must be aware of the discrimination rules, and how fundraising can upset the balance.

PART IV. THE ICING ON TOP 109

12 Wouldn't You Rather Go Out to Eat? 111
Resources to let someone else do the mixing and baking, letting you enjoy the fruits of your labor more.

APPENDICES 115

Appendix A: All your 10-second takeaways in one place 117
Appendix B: Governing document samples 123
Appendix C: IRS registrations and documents 141
Appendix D: Operation guidelines 149
Appendix E: Financial procedure guidelines & templates 167
Appendix F: Fundraising tools 189
Appendix G: Parent Booster USA Model School District Policy 201

PART I

That's a Lot of Cookie Dough!

1

Selling cookie dough is complicated

A few notes about the tangled web of rules and laws that surround the school fundraising "business" without getting into trouble.

It all sounds easy. Sign on with a fundraising company and sell their products to raise money for your school group. Distribute the catalogs and order forms. Order and distribute the products, collect the cash, and walk away with a nice little profit. Of course, you know that getting all the forms and money back is a little tricky. There are always a few stragglers. And motivating busy parents to volunteer can take some doing. But really, selling cookie dough can't be all that complicated, can it?

It can. However, school fundraising is actually a big business, resulting in over $4.5 billion raised each year to supplement the tax dollars that support public education. And, like all businesses, school fundraising is subject to taxes and other government regulation. But unlike other businesses, school fundraising is unique in that it is managed, on a part-time basis, by volunteers with little or no experience or knowledge about fundraising business rules. And one more twist: These groups must contend with close to 100% turnover of their volunteer "staff" each year. Selling cookie dough is really complicated.

Throughout this book I untangle the rules, and provide checklists, tips, and tools to help schools and their volunteers manage the maze of fundraising regulations. Easy as pie, right? (Have you ever tried baking one?)

RECIPE FOR SUCCESS

You may not be getting paid, but everything else about operating a school fundraising group is strictly business. Run it like a boss.

10-SECOND TAKEAWAY

1. School fundraising is big business. Treat it like one!
2. Volunteers are part-time, with little knowledge of the rules.
3. There is close to 100% turnover each year.

2

Selling cookie dough is important

Take a quick minute to pat yourself on the back. What you are doing to support education is important.

Times are tough for public education. Fairfax County Public Schools (FCPS) is projecting a shortfall of up to $100 million by fiscal year 2016. FCPS is looking at reducing or eliminating programs, charging more and higher fees to participate in sports and other extracurricular activities, or finding more non-tax-dollars to fund its programs. That's going to require boosters to sell a lot more cookie dough.

Supplemental funding for education is not new. Bunny Bread built the football stadium in my hometown of Defiance, Ohio. Thanks to Mr. Fred J. Brown, we had the best stadium in Northwest Ohio. There are lots of statistics and studies about the impact of tax dollars and per pupil spending on education, but not much is known about the parent-powered school fundraising industry, including how many groups exist, how much they are raising, and how the contributions of these groups impact the quality of education.

We know that nearly every elementary school in America has a parent teacher organization; most middle schools have one too. Most high schools have numerous fundraising groups, including athletic, music, academic, robotics, and many other booster clubs. Most of these groups, however, are flying under the radar and are operating in violation of local, state and federal fundraising rules. Ever buy a 50/50 raffle ticket at a Friday night football game? Most states have rules that require a license to operate a raffle, and some states prohibit raffles all together. Has your school fundraising group ever filed a tax return? If you raise money, the IRS expects that it be reported.

School Boosters 101 isn't taught to school administrators in grad school. It's the rare parent group that has a nonprofit attorney mom or accountant dad there to help. The result is a multi-billion dollar educational support system run by parents who thought they signed up to sell a little cookie dough to build a new playground, and ended up getting a nastygram from the Internal Revenue Service. These are the school administrators and parents that this book is meant to help.

SOMETHING TO CHEW ON

Harvard professor and author Robert Putnam ("Bowling Alone") talks about the importance of extracurricular activities on student success in his new book, *Our Kids: The American Dream in Crisis,* and laments that "the opportunity gap has widened dramatically ... poor kids are in much worse shape than their counterparts." The growing trend toward sports participation fees in public schools, and the increasing disparity between how much wealthier suburban school booster clubs contribute to extracurricular activities, compared to what is raised and contributed in poorer school districts, is something to chew on.

10-SECOND TAKEAWAY

1. Not much is known about the parent-powered school fundraising industry, including how many groups exist, how much they are raising, and how the contributions of these groups impact the quality of education.
2. We know that most elementary schools in America have a parent teacher organization.
3. Most high schools have numerous fundraising groups, including athletic, music, academic, robotics, and many other booster clubs.
4. Most school fundraising groups are flying under the radar and are operating in violation of local, state and federal fundraising rules.

PART II

Assemble Your Ingredients

In baking, a strong structure is essential.
Otherwise your cookies will go flat.

Sandra Pfau Englund, attorney, amateur baker,
and self-quoting author

3

Structure your group for more success and less risk

The ingredients and a checklist for setting up a school fundraising group.

I get it. You signed up to sell cookie dough or gift wrap, or to organize the concession volunteers for the band boosters. What's all this talk about proper structure and risk?

The reality is that school fundraising is a business. A big business that is subject to a whole slew of federal and state rules and regulations. If you don't know and don't follow the rules, you can get burned. Nobody wants that! Let's get started!

School fundraising groups must be both organized and operated properly. This chapter provides a basic overview of how to structure your school fundraising group for the most credibility and least risk.

Well begun is half done, according to both Aristotle and Mary Poppins, so it must be true. That applies to both tidying the nursery and running a school fundraising group.

Here's a quick checklist on how to set-up your organization:

✔ **Incorporate**. Incorporation provides liability protection for your officers, directors, and volunteers. It also provides additional credibility and a legal entity that may contract for services. To "organize properly" in IRS lingo, and to meet IRS charity rules, you must include special required IRS language in your formation document, the articles of incorporation.

Appendix B provides sample articles of incorporation, including the required IRS language, and tips on how to incorporate your organization.

NOTE: Some school fundraising groups are operated as loose, unincorporated associations of volunteers. While operating this way is legal, I recommend incorporating school fundraising groups due to the liability protection and other benefits.

RECIPE FOR SUCCESS

Don't have a copy of the articles of incorporation and/or are not sure whether your group is incorporated? Most states have a search function on their corporation website, and also allow you to order a copy of your articles of incorporation. To find your state's website, search your state's two-letter abbreviation, followed by a space and then "SOS" (secretary of state). For example, to find the Virginia Secretary of State website, I search [VA SOS]. A listing for the state corporation office should result.

✔ **Check your EIN.** Booster clubs must have their own federal Employer Identification Number (EIN). This number is issued by the Internal Revenue Service and identifies your organization with the IRS on tax returns and other documents. As an independent legal entity, your booster club must have its own EIN and not use the school's.

A link to the IRS application site for an EIN is available at the More than Cookie Dough website: **morecookiedough.com**. Appendix C-1 provides more information about the EIN and how to obtain it. Your EIN is provided in IRS letter CP575.

RECIPE FOR SUCCESS

Keep the CP575 letter in your organization's permanent records. The IRS does not issue replacements.

✔ **Obtain 501(c)(3) tax-exempt status**. All groups that raise money must file the appropriate tax return. If your organization has 501(c)(3) status, it may file the IRS 990-series return and be exempt from paying federal income tax. Good deal! If your group is not a registered 501(c)(3), the IRS expects a corporate tax return. Tax-exempt 501(c)(3) status has many advantages, including allowing your group to receive tax-deductible donations and apply for private foundation and corporate grants. Chapter 5 provides more information on how to obtain tax-exempt status.

A link to the IRS forms page for the 1023EZ and 1023 is available at the More than Cookie Dough website, **morecookiedough.com**. More information about IRS Forms 1023EZ and 1023 is included in Appendices C-2 and C-3.

✔ **Handle state registrations.** Most states require nonprofit groups to register with the state charity agency prior to fundraising. In addition, your group may be eligible to apply for exemption from state sales tax on items purchased in the state for use by your group. Chapter 6 provides more details about state registrations.

A directory of each state's registration requirements is available on the More than Cookie Dough website at **morecookiedough.com**.

Convinced it's more than cookie dough? Mission accomplished! On to the next bite . . . .

10-SECOND TAKEAWAY

1. Incorporating your school fundraising group is highly recommended.
2. To organize properly in IRS lingo means that your formation document (e.g. articles of incorporation) includes all the required IRS language.
3. Make sure to obtain and use your group's own EIN, not the school's.
4. Obtaining 501(c)(3) status offers myriad benefits on both federal and state levels.
5. Federal tax returns must be filed annually, even if your group owes no taxes.
6. Your state has rules, too. Check and follow them!

4

Learn the rules of the game

A brief look at who regulates school fundraising.

In IRS lingo, to "operate properly" means to engage only in activities that support your tax-exempt mission. For most school fundraising groups, supporting their mission involves recruiting volunteers, raising money, and encouraging good communication between the parent group and the school.

Supporting only your tax-exempt activities also means that all of the funds raised must support your mission generally; you may NOT engage in any activities that benefit individual members of your group, including crediting funds raised only to the individual "accounts" of the students who participated in the fundraising activities. What? I know crediting students with funds raised is done all the time, but it's against the IRS rules for 501(c)(3) groups. I'll cover why "cooperative fundraising" is not allowed in Chapter 8.

Let's start with a quick flowchart on the typical annual operations cycle for a school fundraising group, and a brief description of each activity. Subsequent chapters go into more detail.

HOW TO START A SCHOOL FUNDRAISING GROUP

for your booster club

gather your team to help create and distribute tasks

incorperate as a legal entitiy

obtain an **EIN**

budget income and expenses for the year

draft **bylaws**

gain **501(c)(3)** status from the IRS

keep **track** of income and expenses

reconcile the bank account making sure your reports match the bank's reports

report finances to members regularly

pass all of the documents to **new officers** for the next school year

conduct a **yearly review of finances**

1. **Gather your TEAM.** It's important to have a team of officers and other volunteers to spread out the work. Consider having a different volunteer chair each event or activity so no one is asked to take on too much.

Appendix D-1 provides more guidelines for *Recruiting, Training, and Retaining Volunteers*

2. **Review your BYLAWS.** An organization's bylaws provide the rules for how to operate. They usually include duties of the officers and their election process, qualifications for membership, budget guidelines, methods by which funds are appropriated, and detailed financial controls.

Appendix B-2 provides a sample set of bylaws.
A sample set of bylaws also are available at the More than Cookie Dough website, **morecookiedough.com**.
Chapter 7 provides answers to frequently asked questions about bylaws.

3. **Create a BUDGET.** It's important to develop, and have the board and members adopt, a budget for the year's activities. Include in the budget each activity or source of income, and the amount that you expect to raise from each. Also include each type of expense, and the estimated costs. At each meeting,

you should track the budgeted income and estimated expenses against the actual income and expenses. Appendix E provides a sample budget spreadsheet for your use. Chapter 7 provides more detail about how to create and monitor a budget.

A sample budget worksheet is available at the More than Cookie Dough website, **morecookiedough.com**, and also in Appendix E-2.

4. **Check your BANK ACCOUNTS.** You may need to update the signature cards for the organization's bank accounts. In addition, review the EIN used on the bank account; make sure it identifies your group and is not the school's EIN.

5. **Report to your MEMBERS.** Nonprofits should strive for transparency with their members and donors. Membership meetings should include a report on current activities and provide a budget-to-actual report showing income and expenses year-to-date.

A sample budget-to-actual report and balance sheet is available at the More than Cookie Dough website, **morecookiedough.com**.

6. **File all required FEDERAL AND STATE REPORTS, REGISTRATIONS, AND RENEWALS.** Tax-exempt 501(c)(3) groups must file an IRS 990-series return each year to maintain tax-exempt status. Most states require corporations to file an annual report that lists your officers and directors. In addition, many states require renewal of your annual fundraising registration and sales tax exemption certificate. Chapters 5 and 6 provide more details about the reports required and how to file them.

7. **PASS the baton.** Nothing stays the same, especially in school fundraising organizations. Yearly turnover of organization leadership is common. As a result, planning for the turnover, including how to pass along the organization's financial and other history, is critical. Prepare to pass the baton by gathering together your organization's:

   A. Legal documents—articles of incorporation and most recent annual report, bylaws, IRS EIN letter (Form CP575), state registration documents (income and sales tax, fundraising registration);

   B. Financial records—IRS Forms 990, year-end report and statement, year-end internal or external financial report, bank statements and other documents;

   C. Activity records—annual calendar/timeline, annual budget, publicity materials, vendors used, feedback received, ideas for next year.

Appendix D-7 provides a transition checklist.

RECIPE FOR SUCCESS

Using cloud-based document storage and accounting software makes keeping copies your organization's important documents, and keeping track of finances, much easier. In addition, when it comes time to pass the records on, you simply pass on the log-in information and you are done. Learn more about cloud-based tools designed for school fundraising groups in Appendix E. Parent Booster USA makes transitions even easier for its members by providing cloud-based document storage for all key documents and offering state and federal filing services to make sure that you never miss a deadline. More information about PBUSA is provided in Chapter 12, *Wouldn't You Rather Eat Out?*

10-SECOND TAKEAWAY

1. School fundraising groups must be both *organized* and *operated* properly.
2. To be "operated properly" in IRS lingo means that all of your activities, including all the money raised, support your charitable and educational mission; none of your activities may be intended to help individual members of your group raise funds to help pay their personal fees or expenses of participating in the activity.
3. School fundraising groups should be run like a business, including keeping track of the money, and following IRS and state nonprofit fundraising rules.
4. Cloud-based tools for storing important records and documents make transitions of leadership easy.

5

Even school fundraising groups have to file taxes

The IRS wants to jump into the mix when money is involved.

Repeat after me: "**All nonprofits must file federal tax returns.**"

I wanted to put that out there up front, in bold, because it's one of the most widely debated and misunderstood topics I run into as I meet with school administrators and volunteers around the country.

There is a myth that because school fundraising groups support schools, they are free from even filing. At an educational conference for school principals, one attendee was so certain, he challenged me loudly at our trade show booth and stormed away as I tried to explain.

Others believe that smaller nonprofits with gross income of $25,000 or less per year are automatically exempt from filing a tax return or paying taxes. This used to be true, but the law has changed.

Why even nonprofits must file tax returns

A school fundraising group is a small business. Under federal law, all businesses, regardless of income, must file a tax return. Even if your organization is just a loosely organized group of parents and other volunteers that has never incorporated and spends all of its income each year to support an activity at a public high school, the IRS expects a federal income tax return to be filed. If your organization has not been recognized by the IRS as tax-exempt under section 501(c)(3) of the Internal Revenue Code, the IRS expects to get a corporation return, Form 1120.

The confusion over taxes and whether a nonprofit has to file came after a new law was passed. For more than 40 years, prior to the passage of the Pension Protection Act of 2006, nonprofit organizations that raised $25,000 or less each year were not required to file a tax return. The new law, starting in 2008, requires all nonprofits, regardless of funds raised, to file the appropriate tax return. Because most school fundraising groups qualify as 501(c)(3) charitable organizations that are eligible for exemption from paying federal income tax, it's important to get your 501(c)(3) status so you can file a nonprofit, rather than a corporate tax return.

This chapter explains how you can obtain 501(c)(3) status, and then talks more about nonprofit tax returns.

How to file for tax-exempt status (and why you should)

Obtaining federal 501(c)(3) tax-exempt status for your organization is essential to avoiding federal income tax. Federal exemption is also the gateway to state income tax exemption in many states, and often an eligibility requirement for state sales tax exemption. Many grants and grocery or scrip programs require 501(c)(3) status. And only 501(c)(3)s may accept donations deductible on the donor's personal income tax return.

There are two main ways to get a federal exemption:

1. Apply to the IRS using Form 1023-EZ or Form 1023; or
2. Join an umbrella group (such as Parent Booster USA) that can extend its IRS group exemption to your organization.

IRS Forms 1023-EZ and 1023

The original, long-form (12+ pages) 1023 must be used by organizations anticipating annual gross income of $50,000 or more. The long-form 1023 requires attaching the group's governing documents (articles of incorporation and bylaws), budgets for three years, and a laundry list of other information. The form proves difficult, time consuming, and overwhelming for those not experienced with such forms. The IRS filing fee that must accompany paper Form 1023 is $850. IRS review of Form 1023 generally takes six months or more.

A streamlined version of Form 1023, the 1023-EZ, was released by the IRS in July 2014. Five pages shorter than the full Form 1023, the EZ is typically reviewed by the IRS in 60 days or less, and can be completed and filed online for $400 at **pay.gov**. Users of this government website must register and attest that they've read and understand the eligibility requirements and other rules associated with 501(c)(3) organizations. The 1023-EZ makes the exemption process considerably easier for groups that anticipate raising $50,000 or less during each of their first three years of operation.

More information about IRS Forms 1023EZ and 1023 are found in Appendices C-2 and C-3. Links to the forms are available online at the book's companion website, **morecookiedough.com**.

RECIPE FOR SUCCESS

The IRS is now auditing random Form 1023EZ applications, including requiring that most of the information in the Form 1023 be provided to an IRS examiner under a fairly tight deadline. If you file Form 1023EZ, make sure that you have, and keep, your articles of incorporation, bylaws, and a three-year budget in the event the IRS asks for these documents.

Group Exemption

The second option for obtaining 501(c)(3) status is to join an umbrella organization with IRS group exemption authority. When you join an umbrella organization, such as Parent Booster USA (PBUSA)—also known as a "central organization" by the IRS—the central organization registers your group with the IRS. There is no need to complete IRS Form 1023-EZ or 1023 or pay the IRS filing fee. IRS rules provide that the central organization determines your group's eligibility and verifies 501(c)(3) tax-exempt. As a result, exempt status is immediate upon joining.

More information about IRS group exemptions and the immediate tax-exemption joining a group provides is available in IRS Publication 4573, found on the More than Cookie Dough website at **morecookiedough.com**.

Other advantages of joining an umbrella group include the services such groups offer to help your organization maintain tax-exempt status, and educational tools and tips for operating your 501(c)(3) group. Chapter 12, *Wouldn't You Rather Eat Out?* provides more information about the continuity and other benefits of joining a parent organization.

And now more about nonprofit tax returns

Organizations that are recognized by the IRS as 501(c)(3) tax-exempt organizations file the nonprofit tax return, IRS Form 990. There are three different 990 forms—the 990N, 990EZ and the 990—with the appropriate form based on an organization's **gross annual income.**

IRS 990 Filing Requirements for Tax-Exempt Organizations

The nonprofit tax return that you use is based on your annual gross income (before any expenses are deducted) as follows:

990N	Gross receipts normally ≤ \$50,000
990EZ	Gross receipts ≤ \$200,000 and total assets ≤ \$500,000
990	Gross receipts ≥ \$200,000 or total assets ≥ \$500,000

The IRS 990 return is due on the 15th day of the 5th month after the close of an organization's fiscal year that is on record with the IRS. For example, if your organization operates on a school calendar, such as September 1—August 30, the IRS Form 990 is due five months later—on the 15th day of January. **The penalty for failure to file is loss of tax-exempt status!**

RECIPE FOR SUCCESS

If you are not sure of the fiscal year dates that the IRS has on record for your group, you may call the IRS at 1-877-829-5500. You may also check the IRS' Business Master File (BMF) online. A link to the BMF is found on our book website, **morecookiedough.com.** To use the IRS

BMF, you must download the file for your state, and then search by your name or EIN for your record. Your fiscal year end date is found in column "R".

With the turnover of volunteers, your group's fiscal year end date and the 990 due date are often lost from memory, or new volunteers mistakenly change their fiscal year without notifying the IRS. These issues often result in missed or late IRS 990 information returns. Failure to file the appropriate IRS Form 990, on time, for three consecutive years will result in automatic loss of tax-exempt status. Make sure that you mark the date that your 990 is due on the treasurer or group's calendar, and pass this information along to next year's officers. If you qualify to file the online 990N, I recommend that you file it immediately after the close of your fiscal year. In this way, you are less likely to forget to file it, and if there are any issues with the IRS' online filing system, you have five months to handle it.

To change your organization's fiscal year you must notify the IRS on Form 1128. You can't simply change the dates on your tax return. More information on changing your group's fiscal year end is found in Appendix C-4. A link to IRS Form 1128 is found in the bonus material on our companion website, morecookiedough.com.

Filing the 990N *e-Postcard*

If your group normally has annual gross income of $50,000 or less, you may complete the online IRS 990N e-postcard. This electronic filing requires only:

- The organization's name
- Any other names your organization uses (DBAs)
- The organization's mailing address
- The organization's website address (if you have a website)
- The organization's EIN
- The name and address of a principal officer of the organization
- Confirmation of your organization's fiscal year
- Confirmation that your organization's annual gross income is still normally less than $50,000
- Confirmation that your organization has not gone out of business

The 990N eligibility is based on your average or "normal" gross receipts. The IRS website provides that your group qualifies as normally having $50,000 or less in gross annual income if your group:

- Has been in existence for 1 year or less and received, or donors have pledged to give, $75,000 or less during its first taxable year;
- Has been in existence between 1 and 3 years and averaged $60,000 or less in gross receipts during each of its first two tax years; and
- Is at least 3 years old and averaged $50,000 or less in gross receipts for the immediately preceding 3 tax years (including the year for which calculations are being made).

Use the IRS Form 990EZ and 990 to tell your organization's story

IRS Forms 990EZ and the full 990 are an opportunity to tell your members, prospective funders, and the public about the work your organization is doing. The forms filed for the most recent three (3) years must be made available to the public. Your organization's Form 990 should tell all the most important work that you are doing, and provides an opportunity to expand transparency and increase your organization's visibility and credibility.

Here's how:

- Form 990 requires an organization to report your mission and accomplishments for the year. The information that you present should be consistent with information that you publish in your annual report, brochures, website, and other materials.
- Form 990 requires each organization to allocate its expenses between program, administration, and fundraising expenses. When allocating expenses, you should be consistent and accurate; you also should keep in mind that a higher percentage of program expenses-to-overhead expenses (such as administration and fundraising) is looked at more favorably by the public and prospective funders.
- Keep in mind that donors' names and the amount each contributes is confidential information. You should remove this information from your 990 before making the return available to the public.

RECIPE FOR SUCCESS

Federal law requires your organization to make available to the public, upon request, your three most recently filed IRS Forms 990. Archive your 990s, as well as other important documents, in cloud-based document storage for easy retrieval.

What should you do if your group has failed to file tax returns?

If you take over a school fundraising group and discover that it has never filed taxes, what should you do? Have you suddenly become a tax evader? Should you resign immediately and run for the hills?

This is one of those questions for which there is a "right" answer and a "practical" answer. The right answer is that all entities that earn income are required to follow the federal tax laws and file the appropriate tax return. Often, however, filing back tax returns for a school fundraising group that has little, if any, financial records for prior years is difficult or impossible. And, if you file long overdue returns, the group will likely be assessed penalties by the IRS for the past due returns.

While you can't rid the organization of its prior tax liability, you can distance yourself from the prior group's tax issue by dissolving the old entity and starting a new one.

Dissolving the old organization involves five steps:

1. Incorporate a new organization
2. Obtain an Employer Identification Number (EIN) for the new entity
3. Obtain 501(c)(3) status for the new entity
4. Grant any remaining funds from the old entity to the new entity
5. Dissolve the old entity

Each group's tax situation and how to handle missing tax returns is different. That's why this is just something to chew on, and get the advice of a tax or legal professional to decide exactly what to do in your situation.

RECIPE FOR SUCCESS

When starting a new organization, change the organization's name as much as possible. The IRS often "merges" organizations with similar names. This means if the old organization never filed taxes, and the IRS merges your new organization with the old one, you are right back where you started, operating an organization that the IRS believes hasn't filed its tax returns. Getting the IRS to "unmerge" organizations can be a nightmare.

Audits: When the IRS comes calling

While IRS audits of school booster tax returns are fairly rare, it's a good idea to have some knowledge of what the IRS looks for when it reviews tax-exempt organization returns. The IRS commonly looks at five areas in a nonprofit audit: private benefit (are any of the officers, directors or members getting personal financial benefit from the organization's income); commercial activities (is the organization working with a for-profit organization in any capacity and providing too much benefit to the for-profit/commercial entity); has the organization changed its activities from when it obtained tax-exempt status; is the organization engaged in too much lobbying activity or prohibited political activity; and the composition and size of the organization's board of directors, including a review of the board's minutes.

Tips when responding to an audit:

1. **Be brief.** Give the auditor only the information requested and the information that they are entitled to; everything that they ask for may not be necessary to the audit. Only provide information for the specific tax year(s) being audited.
2. **Ask for help.** If concerns about how the audit is being handled come up, contact the auditor's supervisor. In addition, hiring an attorney or tax professional to intervene in the audit often is helpful.
3. **Unsatisfactory results**? Contact the auditor if you cannot understand, or if you disagree with, the examination report. If the result of the audit is unsatisfactory, **it can be appealed** within the IRS and, if still unsatisfactory, to tax court.

Appendix E-6 provides more audit do's and don'ts. The More than Cookie Dough companion website, **morecookiedough.com**, includes a link to IRS publications on audits.

10-SECOND TAKEAWAY

1. All organizations that raise money—including nonprofits—must file an annual federal tax return.
2. Nonprofits seeking tax-exempt charity status must apply to the IRS for 501(c)(3) recognition or obtain 501(c)(3) status under an umbrella group like PBUSA.
3. If your group has failed to file tax returns, dissolve it and start over.
4. If you are faced with an IRS audit, know the rules and ask for help.

6

Your state wants a bite, too!

An outline of what your state government expects to know abut your school fundraising group.

Nobody expects you, as a volunteer in a school support group, to become an expert in nonprofit law—that's my job. The purpose of this book, as the title suggests, is to make it easier for you to navigate these sometimes murky waters; to keep you, and your organization, out of trouble.

In the previous chapters, we discussed what it means to be a nonprofit, the requirements for obtaining and maintaining 501(c)(3) tax-exempt status, and the fact that even tax-exempt organizations are required to file a federal tax return. But that's only half the regulatory picture.

State Regulations

In this chapter, we examine state regulations and registrations.

Incorporation

In Chapter 3, we established that you need to incorporate to obtain tax-exempt status, and while tax exemption applies to both federal and state taxes, incorporation occurs at the state level. Getting incorporated is easier than it used to be. Most states have a simple fill-in form on their Secretary of State's website.

Many states provide a method to file the form either online or via fax. That said, most of the state forms do not include special language the IRS requires for obtaining 501(c)(3) status.

Appendix B-1 provides sample articles of incorporation. The sample highlights the required IRS language and provides a brief explanation of each provision in the articles.

Articles of incorporation use a language all their own. Here's a quick roadmap to help you understand what they mean and how to complete the online forms.

Name: I recommend that you include the abbreviation for incorporated, "Inc." in your name. By including "Inc." in your name, you are putting everyone on notice that your organization is a corporate entity with the liability and protections that incorporation offers.

Purpose: Keep your purpose statement brief and broad. By doing so you decrease the likelihood that you will need to amend the purpose statement in the articles later, requiring another filing with the state. You may define your purpose in more detail in your bylaws. You also need to include the IRS required language about being organized and operated exclusively for 501(c)(3) purposes in this section.

Private benefit: The IRS requires that articles of incorporation for 501(c)(3) groups strictly prohibit any officer, director or member from personal financial gain from the income raised and/or the activities of your organization.

Dissolution: The IRS requires that 501(c)(3) groups contribute any remaining funds when they dissolve to another 501(c)(3) organization or to the government.

Lobbying and political activity: The IRS requires that the articles of incorporation of a 501(c)(3) group include language that limits lobbying activity to the allowable amount, and strictly prohibits political campaign activity.

Registered agent: This is the person to whom the state will send official correspondence. It is often a good idea to name a school staff member—principal, coach, band director—as the registered agent. Every time you change the registered agent you must file a notice with the state. School staff turns over less often than volunteers.

Address: Most states require a street address rather than a P.O. Box on the articles of incorporation. Many groups use the school's address as the official address.

Corporation annual reports

Once your organization has incorporated, most states require that a corporate report be filed each year listing the group's current officers and address. Some states allow the forms to be filed online; others require a paper form be signed and returned. Most states require an annual fee. Many states assess a modest penalty for late filing.

Often, failure to file for two or more years will result in the loss of corporate status. Unless too many years go by, corporate status usually may be restored by filing the late annual reports and paying the required filing fees and penalties. Due dates for corporate annual reports vary by state. Some are based on an organization's fiscal year; others are based on the date the IRS 990 annual report is due; still others have a unique filing date all their own.

Income and franchise taxes

Some states automatically exempt organizations incorporated within the state as nonprofit corporations from state income tax. Others require a separate application for state income tax exemption. The same applies to state franchise taxes.

Fundraising registration

Most states require nonprofit organizations to register with the state charities division, usually housed within the state attorney general's office, **prior to raising funds from the public**. State laws vary, but many have exceptions for groups that raise less than a specified dollar amount or seek donations only from their own members and not from the general public.

Once registered, most states require groups to renew their registration annually. Renewal typically requires filing a report that lists total funds raised, whether any professionals were used to help with fundraising, and the like. Often, there is a renewal fee. Failure to file typically results in fees and penalties.

Sales tax

In states with a sales tax, organizations with 501(c)(3) status may often (but not always) apply for exemption from paying sales tax on items purchased for use by the organization. Sales tax laws are complex, and vary widely throughout the United States. Some states provide exemption only on certain items. Others provide sales tax exemptions only in very limited cases.

There are two components to sales tax—the tax you pay when purchasing items; and the tax you must collect when selling items. School fundraising groups that sell spirit wear, for example, may need to collect and pay sales tax on the items sold. Again, the variations are numerous.

Some states allow a certain number of tax-free sale days on which a group is not required to collect and pay sales tax. Other states provide exemptions from sales tax for some items—such as the sale of concessions at sports events, or the sale of an annual yearbook—but require sales tax be collected and paid on other items.

A link to a complete list of state tax requirements is found on our companion site at **morecookiedough.com**.

Increasing regulation makes fundraising a daunting task

The federal and state paperwork burden for nonprofits is fairly steep and seems to keep getting steeper. Since the passage of the Pension Protection Act of 2006, Tennessee enacted the School Support Organization Financial Accountability Act in 2007, based on a perceived need to ensure stronger financial accountability of school fundraising groups.

In 2012, Ohio revised its fundraising registration rules to require school support groups that were previously exempt from registering to file reports. What makes operating a school support "business" particularly tricky is the rapid turnover of their "staff" or volunteers. With no corporate history, ensuring that each year's new officers know and understand the rules, filing, and registration requirements is almost impossible.

RECIPE FOR SUCCESS

I founded Parent Booster USA in 2004 because I knew then that schools and parent volunteers needed help handling the increasing regulation of fundraising, and the continuous turnover of parent volunteers operating school fundraising groups. More about PBUSA is found in Chapter 12, *Wouldn't You Rather Eat Out?*

10-SECOND TAKEAWAY

1. Incorporation happens at the state level and usually requires a fee and an annual corporate report identifying officers and contact information.
2. State taxes, including income, franchise and sales tax, are separate from federal tax and require separate applications for exemption.
3. Most states now require nonprofit groups to register prior to starting a fundraising campaign in the state.

7

Tools & tidbits to make things easier

Notes, tips, and templates to help you handle your money, run your meetings, and limit your risks.

Bylaws

The rules of how your group operates, including when and how officers are elected, voting rights of the members, and how often meetings are held, are included in your group's bylaws. State law generally requires that nonprofit corporations have a set of bylaws. Sometimes the rules in your bylaws may change what is provided in state law. For example, you typically have the ability to set the minimum number of people that makeup a quorum to transact business. If you don't include a quorum provision in your bylaws, the state law provision applies. Other state requirements, however, such as the minimum number of people who must serve on your board of directors, cannot be changed by a provision in your bylaws.

Not having a set of bylaws, or not being allowed to review the bylaws your school fundraising group has in place, is a red flag. This may happen if the prior bylaws simply got lost. If this is the case, it's time to write new bylaws. Sometimes, when one or a few people are attempting to maintain total control of an organization, it may be difficult to get a copy of the bylaws. You may want to make the officers aware that state nonprofit laws generally require that an organization's bylaws be made available to all the members of the group.

RECIPE FOR SUCCESS

Make it a practice to review your bylaws before you start the year's activities. Make sure the bylaws reflect how you are actually operating the organization, and that all members of your group have a copy of the bylaws, or access to them by making them available on your group's website.

A complete sample set of bylaws with annotations regarding each provision is included in Appendix B-2.

Here are some frequently asked questions about bylaw rules:

Should a school staff member serve on the group's board?

It's a good idea to have a school staff member serve as an advisory, non-voting, member of the group's board. Working closely with your school is an essential part of being a "support" organization. Nevertheless, the relationship between the fundraising group and the school should be viewed as grantor (fundraising group) to grantee (school). Therefore, the school should advise the fundraising group about its needs and operations, but should not vote.

How often should the board meet? The members?

State law generally requires very few meetings. However, most school parent teacher organizations and booster clubs meet with the members once a month; the officers often meet more frequently.

Who is entitled to vote?

Typically members of a school fundraising group have voting rights and vote on key decisions including the annual budget, amendments to the budget, key programs and activities to be undertaken, and how funds will be spent (grants to the school). Sometimes the officers will vote between membership meetings on expenditures included within the approved budget and other routine matters. I recommend that school staff serve as advisory, non-voting members of the group.

RECIPE FOR SUCCESS

Fundraising groups that support for-profit "schools," such as competitive cheerleading and gymnastics gyms, must be especially careful to separate the activities of the school and its activities to support competitive athletics. Gym owners should NEVER vote on matters brought before the booster club. In addition, the booster club must NEVER pay for any expenses that directly help the bottom line of the for-profit gym.

What type of financial policies should we have?

The financial policies are among the most important sections of the bylaws. It is essential to include strong policies that require your group to operate like a business, including requiring two people to count cash, two people to sign checks, and two people to reconcile the bank account. (See discussion of theft and financial controls below.) All nonprofit groups also should require an audit committee to conduct a financial review each year.

Budgets

Getting a volunteer to serve as the treasurer of a school fundraising group can be a hard sell. Your school is lucky if a parent steps forward who has accounting or bookkeeping experience. Have a CPA volunteer? Count your lucky stars.

But managing the finances of your school fundraising group doesn't have to be an impossible, thankless job, provided you employ the latest tools and follow some simple guidelines. Here's my 5-step no-fail (okay—no guarantees—but I'm doing my best here) financial management plan:

Step 1: Budget. Get your officers together and develop a budget for the full school year. A simple spreadsheet like the one pictured below works well. First, list each planned fundraising event or income-producing activity down the left column. Then enter how much you hope to raise from each activity to the right of each item. When you list expected income in a budget it should be the total (gross) amount that you expect to raise before expenses are taken out.

INCOME		
Individual donations	$1,000	
Fall festival	$10,000	
Cookie dough sale	$5,000	
Car washes (4 total)	$1,000 ($250/car wash)	
TOTAL INCOME		**$17,000**

Next, list your expenses. These include the amount of money that you will donate to the school for various activities, equipment, transportation and other items. Again, list each expense down the left, and the expected amount of the expense to the right. For each income item for which there is a cost (printing fair share donation request letters, fall festival expenses) there should be a related expense item listed.

EXPENSES		
Individual donation campaign costs	$100	
Fall festival expenses	$1,000	
Cookie dough cost of goods sold	$2,500	
Car wash expenses	$100	
Playground fund grant	$9,500	
Library grant	$1,500	
Teacher appreciation day	$300	
TOTAL EXPENSES		**$15,000**
NET (Carry-over)		**$2,000**

RECIPE FOR SUCCESS

I'm often asked if fundraising groups must spend all money raised during the year in the year it was raised. The answer is no. There is no rule or law against carrying over income to start the next year. In fact, many larger nonprofits with paid staff will try to set aside reserve funds in an amount that would cover 6-12 months operating expenses. Larger projects, such as a new playground, might require you to set aside funds for several years before the total required amount is raised. The same is true for marching bands that plan to go on big trips, or athletic boosters that raise money to replace uniforms every three years. Setting up start-up funds for next year's officers, and planning for bigger expenses over several years, is both legal under IRS fundraising rules and a good way to do business.

Step 2. Track. The treasurer should keep track of all income and expenses, including attaching invoices and receipts to transactions. At each meeting, the treasurer should provide a budget-to-actual report that shows how well you are actually doing compared to your budget plan.

You can use a simple spreadsheet and make a report such as the one below. However, I recommend using one of the many different online cloud-based accounting software packages. Not only does accounting software make the job easier, and more accurate, it also allows you pass the financial information on to next year's treasurer easily. Simply pass on the log-in information and you're done.

More about cloud-based accounting software is included in Appendix E-7.

Sample Year End Budget-to-Actual Report

	BUDGET July 1, 2015—June 30, 2016	ACTUAL-TO-DATE[2] June 1, 2016
INCOME		
Individual donations	$1,000	$1,500
Fall festival	$10,000	$12.000
Cookie dough sale	$5,000	$4,250
Car washes	$1,000	$750
TOTAL INCOME	**$17,000**	**$18,500**
EXPENSES		
Individual donation campaign	$100	$82.56
Fall festival	$1,000	$1,119.00
Cookie dough sale	$2,500	$2,125.00
Car washes	$100	$92.00
Playground fund	$9,500	$9,500
Library grant	$1,500	$2,500
Teacher Appreciation Day	$300	$312
TOTAL EXPENSES	**$15,000**	**$14,730.56**
Carry Over	**$2,000**	**$3,769.44**

In the above example, the group has a net carryover of $3,769.44 against a budgeted amount of $2,000. The group may consider taking a vote to decide how to use the extra $1,769.44. They could, for example, decide to set the extra amount aside in the playground fund, increase the size of the library grant, or simply leave all the funds for the following year.

Step 3. Reconcile. It's important to reconcile your books to the bank's records each month. Using accounting software makes this task much easier.

Step 4. Report. A report, including the bank balance and reconciliation, and budget-to-actual report should be presented at each meeting. A reluctance on the part of a treasurer or other officer to make financial records available for review or a failure to routinely report on income and expenses are both bad practices, and may be red flags that the books are not in order.

Step 5. Review. A financial review should be conducted each year. The review may be done internally—until your gross receipts exceed $250,000—by volunteers. The volunteers conducting the annual review are providing additional oversight for your finances and therefore should not have been involved in the day-to-day financial management of your organization, including for example having bank signature authority or expense approval authority.

RECIPE FOR SUCCESS

The Better Business Bureau's Charity Division sets standards for who may conduct the annual financial review based on the gross income of an organization as follows:

Gross income	Review may be conducted
Less than $250,000	Internally by volunteers without signature or routine banking authority
$250,000—$499,999	Compilation review (less than a full audit) by an outside certified professional accountant (CPA)
$500,000+	Full audit by outside CPA

The Better Business Bureau's Charity Division rules are all found at **give.org**.

Step-by-step guidelines on how volunteers can conduct an internal financial review are included in Appendix E-5.

Theft & financial controls

Unfortunately, theft is a common problem in school fundraising groups, likely because the trust level is high and business and financial controls are not in place, or are not followed. More than one case of school fundraising theft is reported in the news each week, with well over $1 million stolen each year. You can reduce the risk of theft substantially by following these three simple rules:

1. **Cash controls—never count cash alone.** Two people should always be present to count cash. Cash should be counted on-site where it's collected. A cash tally sheet, signed by the counters, should be used to record the totals. Cash should then be immediately deposited into the bank.

2. **Checks—two people should be required to sign checks.** This requirement should be printed on the organization's checks and strictly adhered to. **Never pre-sign blank checks!**

3. **Bank statements—two sets of eyes on the bank statements.** A second person, without signature authority, should reconcile bank statements. It's a good idea to require the bank statements, reconciliation reports, deposit slips, and cash tally sheets to be kept together and made available at meetings for review.

With proper organization, operations, and controls, your fundraising group should be well on its way toward a successful and pain-free year. And while there are bound to be challenges in any endeavor where people and their varying interests, priorities, and feelings are involved, you'll at least be assured that the business side of the house is in order.

SOMETHING TO CHEW ON...

What happens when one person is left alone to count cash? In a Nebraska high school, the result was that one mom walked away with a lot of cash over a two-year period. "Mary" was convicted of stealing $14,000 from the school spirit store where she volunteered. At first she said she didn't know why she did it. After years of therapy, Mary says she's learned that she has a shopping addiction, a type of kleptomania and that, in the end, it was a relief to get caught.

This is not an isolated case. Parent Booster USA began tracking school fundraising theft in early 2015 and discovered that at least one new case a week is being reported. Why do people steal from kids? That's a good question, but perhaps we should be asking why school fundraising groups are the victims of so much theft.

In Mary's case there were no checks and balances in the booster club spirit shop where she volunteered. The cash register did not print out a daily total-collected amount. The money was just put in the register, and Mary was left alone to count the cash and make the bank deposit. The booster club's bylaws provided that two people were required to sign checks, but the policy was never enforced, because it was considered to be too time-consuming.

As Mary was paying her debt to society, another case of embezzlement surfaced 1,300 miles away in Connecticut. The treasurer of an elementary school PTO had been charged with stealing more than $45,000. According to the school district superintendent, "Eight mothers came to my office in tears. The treasurer had been their friend; they trusted her."

Strong and consistently applied financial controls allow volunteers to maintain friendly trust, and run the school fundraising group like a business.

RECIPE SIDEBAR

Too often I see groups include sound financial rules in their bylaws, and then fail to enforce the rules as soon as someone complains that getting a second person to count the cash or sign the checks is too hard. "Don't you trust us?" is a common refrain. Trust has nothing to do with it. In the eyes of the IRS and state government, operating a school fundraising group is the same as operating a business, only with more scrutiny, because it involves donations. Strong financial controls protect everyone—the group, the public, and the people counting the cash.

Meeting management

Recently I attended an elementary school parent teacher organization meeting. Only about a half-dozen parents, in addition to the four officers, showed up. The officers lamented that this was the usual turnout, because it left them with most of the work. There are many reasons for limited support of school fundraising groups. Some—conflicting obligations, two career families with limited spare time—are difficult to solve. Nevertheless, there are a few key ways to gain more support for your meetings, and for your group's activities.

1. **Don't meet just to meet.** Just because the middle school band boosters have always met once a month in the past doesn't mean you have to keep up the practice. Only meet if there is reason—meaning you have decisions to make that require the input of the members. Tell the members in the meeting notice what topics you will be discussing and/or what items will be voted upon.

The PTO meeting I attended was merely a recitation by the officers on the budget and events. The members were not asked for any input. There was nothing to vote on. In this day of busy lives and easy communication via websites and email, the information shared at this meeting could have been shared electronically.

2. **Meet at a convenient time.** When setting a meeting date and time, think about the parents you hope will attend. Do you have largely two-career families or working single parents? If so, meeting in the evening will allow them to attend. Are there a large number of stay-at-home or work-at-home parents in your school district? Then a morning meeting right after the kids are dropped at school, or an afternoon meeting right before the kids are released, may work. Or consider alternating between school day and evening meetings, and providing child care, to help everyone attend.

When my son was in the high school band, booster club meetings were always held on Monday nights. The high school had a magnet music program, meaning many students lived a long distance from the school. Parents were already driving their kids to and from school, and back to school for band practice Tuesday and

Thursday nights. Parents who were already investing 12 hours or more commuting to the high school had no desire to return again on a Monday night. Holding the meetings on Tuesday nights right before, during, or after the band rehearsal, when the parents had to be at school anyway, would have been more convenient, and likely garnered greater attendance.

3. **Use an agenda. Start and end on time**. Using an agenda, and starting and ending on time, shows people that you value their time. It also lends a more business-like approach to meetings. Include start/end times for each topic as well, such as allotting 20 minutes per topic. This works particularly well for controversial topics where you allow each person to speak only once to allow everyone who wants to contribute to the discussion has the opportunity to speak.

Suggestions for managaing meetings are included in Appendices D-2 and D-3.

4. **Minutes should record only actions taken**. Meeting minutes should be thought of as a record of actions taken, not a recording of the discussions at the meeting. Contrary to the common belief that minutes are taken to advise the members not in attendance what happened at the meeting, minutes are actually a legal record of the actions taken at the meeting. Because minutes are required to be kept by law, and can be requested by the IRS in an audit or a court in a legal action, minutes should include only a brief description of actions on which a vote was

taken, and the result (passed/failed, and not the vote count). Keep the play-by-play description for verbal conversations with any members who could not attend the meeting.

See Appendix D for meeting guidelines, including *Tips and Strategies to Run Great Meetings, sample minutes,* and *ParliPro Basics for Conducting a Meeting.*

Program planning & volunteer management

Too often the bulk of the work in school fundraising groups falls on the shoulders of the elected officers. It's no wonder that recruiting new officers can be difficult. Here are a couple of ways to help manage your programs, and recruit more volunteers.

1. **Seek volunteers for specific programs/projects of limited duration.** Instead of having a Vice President for Fundraising, consider seeking a volunteer for each program—a car wash chair, a cookie dough sale chair, silent auction chair, etc. You may even be able to recruit more volunteers if you subdivide: a different chair for each car wash, for example; or task-specific assignments for each component of the silent auction—set-up, classroom basket table, and so forth.

2. **Ask for a reasonable amount of time.** Suggest that each football, band, softball, or robotics parent contribute five hours for the full year, and provide a list of volunteer options to choose from. Ask parents to chaperone just one away game or event.

Busy parents shy away from volunteering for what may appear to be a never-ending assingment.

3. **Make friends.** The group's officers should warmly welcome new volunteers. Twice recently, parents told me that they actively participated at one school, but not at the next grade level because officers made them feel as if their help wasn't wanted. Openly encouraging discussion of topics at meetings, sharing and voting on the group's annual program plan, and providing lots of different volunteer opportunities encourages greater participation, and more success.

Advice on calls for volunteers is included in Appendix D-1.

Permission Slips

If you have children, I'm sure that you've signed a few permission slips in your day, asking that you hold the school and its staff blameless for anything that might happen to your child while on a field trip or other activity off school grounds. You signed away, to make sure that your child could go on the trip and not be left idling at the school. The reality is that signing your name on the line likely did not sign away your, or your child's, rights if he or she got hurt. Courts are reluctant to uphold broadly written permission slips. The reason? Courts have ruled that parents can not give up rights to keep their child safe by signing overly broad permission slips that do not fully describe the nature of the activity and its risks. How do you make a permission slip stick? There's no iron-clad way (if I controlled all the judges in the land, I probably wouldn't be writing this book!). Nevertheless, here are a few tips.

1. **Details, details, details**. Include as much detail as possible in the permission slip regarding each of the activities in which the students will engage. For example, if the elementary children are going to a petting zoo, include how the children will be transported (school bus? chaperones' personal vehicles?), the activities at the zoo (introduced to animals including rabbits, goats, cows and chickens; eat a packed lunch at the zoo picnic grounds; have time to climb on the zoo's playground; and take part in a zoo scavenger hunt in which groups of 3-4 children and a chaperone hunt for clues throughout the zoo's indoor and outdoor exhibits and race to be the first one to complete the task.)

2. **The risks**. Spell out the likely and most common risks of the students participating in the activity. For example, common risks of outdoor activities include insect bites (including bee stings and mosquito bites), and sun, rain and other weather exposure. (Animal risks include possible bites, kicks, or other reactions of the animals to the children.)

3. **Insurance.** Require parents to have appropriate medical insurance coverage for their children.

4. **Medical treatment**. Ask parents to grant the school and chaperones permission to seek appropriate medical treatment for the children if necessary if a parent cannot be reached.

5. **Contact numbers**. Require two or more phone numbers to reach the parents, guardians, or others who may grant permission for treatment or care if an emergency arises.

A sample permission slip is included in Appendix D-6.

Insurance & risk management

It's all good and fine until someone gets hurt. That little parenting gem certainly applies when it comes to protecting your booster club, and its officers, from lawsuits arising from mishaps at otherwise fun events. When kids get hurt, parents sue!

A child breaks her leg playing pick-up soccer at an ice-cream social; a ticket booth collapses, injuring a volunteer; a referee twists an ankle at a charity volleyball tournament. These are some real life examples of lawsuits filed against school fundraising groups.

Imagine some other likely scenarios: What if the band uniforms get lost or damaged before they are paid for? What if a football player gets sick from eating a booster-sponsored pregame meal? What if a student sneaks alcohol into a PTO-sponsored event and dies, or is injured?

As with so many other common misconceptions involving SSOs, a lot of volunteers assume that the organization is covered under the school's insurance. In fact, most school insurance does not cover the activities of outside organizations, like school fundraising groups. As a result, it is strongly recommended that you carry insurance protection for your group.

There are four basic types of insurance that nonprofit organizations typically carry:

1. **General Liability**—to cover accidents and injuries to individuals;
2. **Directors and Officers (D&O)**—to cover the personal liability of officers and directors for their legal responsibilities serving the organization;
3. **Property**—to cover loss of property/assets of the organization, such as damage to facilities, owned and rented equipment, and property/inventory related to fundraising programs (the wrapping paper, candy or other products that the parent group receives before they are distributed and funds collected); and,
4. **Bonding**—to cover loss of funds of the organization to embezzlement and the like.

Insurance is just one way to handle the potential liability of operating a school fundraising group. The other key way to limit your risks is to put in place a risk management program, and transfer or place the risks of your activities on the party (e.g., school, outside vendor) that is most able to manage the risk. A basic risk-management system can be developed following these simple steps:

Identify the most likely risks

Think about the activities your group is planning this year and the most likely risks involved. Will you be having a fall festival with pony rides and a slip-n-slide? These activities could result in personal injuries. Will you be sponsoring field trips including transporting students off campus? This, too, could lead to personal injuries. Are you purchasing equipment or uniforms? Or are you selling wrapping paper, cookie dough or some other item? If so, you could be liable for property damage, if for example, the equipment, uniforms, or merchandise is damaged after you receive it, but before it is granted to the school or distributed to those who bought the fundraising merchandise. Do you handle cash and other funds? Theft, unfortunately, happens. And officers and directors may be liable for managing the operations of the group.

Assess the risks and modify as appropriate

Decide if an activity is so important to your mission that you must tolerate the risk. Other activities may be modified to reduce the risk, or eliminated, if the risk outweighs the benefit of continuing the activity.

Control for the risks

This means that you avoid risks that are too great to bear, and modify policies, plans, and procedures to reduce risks where you can. Controlling for the risks also includes transferring risks to others where appropriate, including the use of informed consent documents (aka permission slips), by contractual agreement, and through insurance.

For example, make sure your contract with the pony ride vendor provides that the pony ride operator is responsible for all injuries, rather than the parent teacher organization. Same goes for contracts with bus companies or other transportation providers. The transportation company, and not the booster club, should be liable for safe driving. In other cases, the school, rather than the fundraising group, should be making the purchase of the uniforms or equipment and therefore be responsible for loss or damage.

RECIPE FOR SUCCESS

The best way to handle the school and school fundraising group relationship is for the school fundraising group to focus on raising funds to supplement the school budget, and grant funds to the school to purchase the supplies or contract for needed. School staff generally have more experience with vendors and contracting. This approach also greatly reduces the volunteer group's risks.

10-SECOND TAKEAWAY

1. Bylaws should reflect how you actually operate. Update them as needed.
2. School staff commonly should be advisory, non-voting members of school fundraising groups.
3. Preparing an annual budget, and implementing good financial practices and controls is essential.
4. Meetings should start and end on time, and provide an opportunity for input by those present. Meeting minutes should record only the actions taken and not details about the discussion.
5. Permission slips must be detailed and specific to allow parental consent that a court will uphold.
6. Most school insurance policies don't cover school fundraising groups. You need your own coverage.

PART III

More Food for Thought

8

Fundraising do's and don'ts

Deductions rules, donations receipts, and raffle rules all in one place.

As the mother of three kids, I've participated in more school, scout, dance, church, and other fundraisers than I can count. My least favorite were the fundraisers that tried to entice the kids to sell more by offering a prize. I still have a huge stack of car visor-size write-on white boards my son convinced me to buy so he'd have 60 seconds inside a glass box blowing money around. I'm sure I spent far more on the white boards that I never found any use for than my son Drew won in the money machine!

With school budgets running deficits, fundraising is likely to become more common than less. This chapter outlines some of the key IRS and state rules governing fundraisers.

> More fundraising resources including a quick reference guide to the rules, best practices running a fundraiser, sample donation request letter, cash/in-kind donation form, and donor receipt provided in Appendix F.

What's deductible, What's not

One of the key benefits of getting your school fundraising group recognized as a tax-exempt 501(c)(3) educational and charitable group is that voluntary donations to your group are tax-deductible to the donor. With 501(c)(3) status you can offer the "no-fund-raiser" fundraiser currently growing in popularity.

THE NO-MORE-COOKIE-DOUGH, NO-MORE-SILENT AUCTION, NO TIME FOR THAT FUNDRAISER

No time to bake? No time to volunteer? Tired of buying and selling cookie dough and gift wrap? This is the fundraiser for you! Just fill out this form and we won't ask for any more support the rest of the school year!

$15 Here's the money I would have spent baking the cakes for the fall festival cake walk.

$25 Here's the money I would have spent on gift wrap that I don't need.

$50 Please excuse me from the walk or run or swim or any other "thon" planned for the year.

$75 I'm happy to contribute this instead of dressing up the for fancy silent auction and ball.

$________ I'm contributing this in grateful appreciation for being able to support the school, my kids, and their teachers without taking on another part-time job of fundraising!

Student name ______________________ Grade ____

Your name ________________________________

Email ____________________________________

Thank you for support of the All American Elementary School and our "no-fundraiser" fundraiser!

As a 501(c)(3) organization, your contribution to the school PTO is tax-deductible. We will email you a receipt for your tax records.

Contributions to the no-fundraiser fundraiser are tax-deductible, because they are (1) made to a school fundraising organization that has obtained 501(c)(3) tax-exempt status, (2) the donor is making the contribution voluntarily, and (3) the donor receives nothing in return for the contribution except the satisfaction of supporting the school.

Common mistakes I see with these types of fundraisers include:

1. The school fundraising group states that contributions are tax-deductible but the organization is not recognized by the IRS as a 501(c)(3) charitable organization. Simply supporting a school is not enough to cause an organization be tax-exempt. The group must apply for, obtain, and then maintain its 501(c)(3) status.
2. The contribution is not really voluntary. Often fees required to participate in an activity are described as contributions. If the fee is actually required, or if parents are led to believe that payment is required, the payment is not voluntary, and therefore is not a tax-deductible contribution.
3. Something of value is received in return for the contribution. My favorite was when I saw a local service club advertise tax-deductible Christmas trees. The reality is that whether you pay $35 for your Christmas tree from the local hardware store, or $35 for a tree from your local 501(c)(3) service club, you still got a $35 Christmas tree. That's a purchase, not a donation.

Let's look at how a $100 payment to the All American High School Band can be a tax-deductible contribution, or a non-deductible fee, depending on the circumstances:

The voluntary band donation

A band parent writes a check for $100 made out to the All American High School Band Parent Boosters and hands it to the band director, saying, "I know you never have enough funds to buy all the instruments and music that you need to run the band. Here's a donation to help."

This is a tax-deductible, voluntary donation for which the donor received nothing in return for the contribution.

Another voluntary band donation

A band parent writes a check for $100 made out to the All American High School Band Parent Boosters and hands it to the band director, saying, "I know you never have enough funds to buy all the instruments and music that you need to run the band. Here's a donation to help."

The band director runs to his office and grabs a plastic kazoo emblazoned with the words, *All American High School Band,* hands it to the parent and says, "Thanks for your contribution to the band program. Here's a kazoo. Bring it to all the football games and play it loudly when the band is announced before performing its half-time show."

This is a tax-deductible, voluntary donation even though the donor received the kazoo as a thank-you gift for the contribution. The receipt of any item that is considered "de minimus," or a token, does not change the deductibility of the gift.

The partial band donation

A band parent writes a check for $100 made out to the All American High School Band Parent Boosters and hands it to the band director, saying, "Here's my fair share contribution to support the band this year. I really appreciate that you are giving me a new band parent polo shirt this year as a thank-you gift for contributions of $100 or more."

The fair market value of the polo shirt (what it would cost to buy at the high school spirit store) is $25. Therefore, this is a tax-deductible contribution of $75. The remaining $25 of the payment is considered payment for the polo shirt received in exchange for the contribution.

The band fee

A band parent writes a check for $100 made out to the All American High School Band Parent Boosters and hands it to the band director, saying, "Here's our payment for band camp for Mary."

This is a fee paid to allow Mary to participate in band camp. It is not tax-deductible.

RECIPE FOR SUCCESS

A thank-you gift is considered a token if the fair market value of the thank-you gift does not exceed the lesser of 2% of the donation amount, or $105*; or if the only items provided are ones that bear the organization's name and/or logo, with a cost equal to or less than the IRS low-cost item amount ($10.50*).

*the values provided are for the year 2015; values are adjusted annually for inflation.

IRS publication 1771, Charitable Contributions, provides more information about substantiation and disclosure requirements. A link to this and other IRS publications is found at the More than Cookie Dough companion website, **morecookiedough.com**.

What about auctions?

Many school fundraising groups hold silent or live-bidding auctions to raise money. Generally a donor of products and services to a fundraising auction is limited to taking a deduction of the donor's cost or tax-basis in the donated property. People who purchase items at the auction generally may take a charitable deduction only if they can document that the price paid exceeded the fair market value of the item purchased. Otherwise, the purchaser is considered to have received something of value in return for the payment and therefore has not made a voluntary contribution.

RECIPE FOR SUCCESS

Your group may want to indicate the fair market value of each item for sale at the auction, and let participants know that, to the extent their winning bids exceed the listed fair market value, they may take a tax-deductible contribution.

Are business sponsorships deductible?

I often see fundraising groups soliciting local businesses to sponsor their sport or other activity. Frequently the sales flyers state that payments made are tax-deductible. Generally this is not the case because the businesses that make these payments receive advertising in exchange for their payments. Here are a few examples of what is, and is not, an advertising expense rather than a tax-deductible contribution.

Sporting goods store pays to sponsor the football team

The local sporting goods store sponsors the All American High School Football Boosters. In exchange for the store's payment of $500, the store receives a printed banner to hang at the football stadium, a half-page ad in the football program, and at least two promotional announcements during each home football game.

This is advertising. While the payment may be deductible by the sporting goods store as a business advertising expense, it is not deductible as a charitable donation because of the advertising that the store receives in return for its payment.

Sporting goods store pays to sponsor the football team

The local sporting goods store sponsors the All American High School Football Boosters. In exchange for the store's payment of $500, the store is listed in the football program as a "gold" sponsor. All "gold" sponsors are announced at half-time during home football games as supporting the team.

This payment may be considered a tax-deductible donation because the recognition that the store receives is within the boundaries of IRS "qualified sponsorship" rule and is not considered advertising.

RECIPE FOR SUCCESS

In addition to your sponsors not getting a tax-deduction for advertising payments, 501(c)(3) tax-exempt organizations must report and pay tax at corporate rates on their net income from advertising. As a result, it is important to keep track of your gross income from advertising sales, and also your expenses related to the advertising sales, for example the cost to print and hang the banners in the stadium and the cost to print the football programs.

IRS QUALIFIED SPONSORSHIP RULES

Permissible recognition (payments made are tax-deductible to donor; income is tax-exempt to the organization):

1. sponsor logos and slogans that do not contain comparative or qualitative descriptions of the sponsor's product, services, facilities or company;
2. sponsor locations/addresses and telephone numbers;
3. value-neutral descriptions, including displays or visual depictions, of a sponsor's product line or services; and
4. sponsor brand or trade names and product or service listings.

Recognition considered "advertising" (may be deductible for donor as business expense but not charitable deduction; is taxable to the tax-exempt organization to extent proceeds exceed related costs.)

1. qualitative or comparative language about a sponsor's products, services, facilities or company;
2. price information or other indications of savings or value associated with a product or service;
3. an endorsement;
4. an inducement to purchase, sell or use the sponsor's products or service (however, distribution of a sponsor's product to the public at a sponsored event, whether for free or for charge, would not be considered an inducement to purchase, sell or use the product);
5. the amount of the payment contingent on the attendance level at one or more events, broadcast ratings, or other factors indicating the degree of public exposure (although a payment contingent on the mere occurrence of an event or its broadcast would not, for that reason alone, be subject to Unrelated Business Income Tax (UBIT)).

RECIPE FOR SUCCESS

Advise your business sponsors that their payments may be deductible as a business expense by stating for example, *"Thank you for your support of our school booster organization. Your contribution may be deductible as a business advertising expense based on the recognition you will receive."* Or alternatively, if some, but not all of the payment is for advertising, *"Thank you for your support of our school booster organization. One half of your payment, $250, is considered a tax-deductible contribution in support of our program. The remaining half of your payment may be deductible as a business advertising expense based on the recognition that you will receive for your payment."*

Receipts

IRS rules require that organizations receiving donations provide a written receipt disclosing the portion of a contribution that is tax-deductible for all gifts of $75 or more. IRS rules also require that donors have written documentation of their donations in order to claim a tax deduction. A receipt from the charity is required for all donations of $250 or more. A copy of a check, bank record or other documentation is enough for smaller contributions.

Receipts should include:

- Name of the organization
- Amount of a cash contribution, or value of an in-kind contribution

- Statement regarding whether goods or services were received in exchange for the payment
- Good faith estimate of the value of any goods or services that were received in exchange for the donation, if any

The receipt may be a paper document, or an electronic acknowledgement. A receipt may be provided for each donation throughout the year, or one annual statement of all contributions made by the same donor throughout the year may be provided.

RECIPE FOR SUCCESS

Keeping records of donors and donations made is not only a requirement of the IRS, but an essential business practice of nonprofit organizations. Commonly, prior donors become future donors; smaller donors become larger donors.

Games of Chance

Recently I heard about a high school booster club in Ohio that set-up what they thought was a fun and innovative fundraiser. Participants buy a square on a board that corresponds with a score at a milestone of an Ohio State football game. Guess correctly and winners receive a percentage of the pot. The problem is that booster club was supposed to get a license from the state of Ohio prior to operating the fundraiser which is considered a "game of chance."

Under Ohio law, games of chance include any kind of game in which money is paid with a chance to win a prize. This type of gambling may only be conducted in Ohio by organizations recognized as 501(c)(3)s, that have been in continuous existence for at least two years, and take place on premises owned by the organization for at least a year, or leased from a governmental agency. In addition, these types of games of chance cannot be held more than five days in a calendar year. This high school booster club not only did not obtain a license, but was not eligible for one because it had been in existence less than two years.

It's not only Ohio that regulates games of chance. Many states require a license for any activity in which money is paid for a chance to win a prize. Games of chance include raffles and bingo. As a result, before you start a 50/50 raffle or another game of chance, check the specific rules for your state.

Cooperative fundraising—everybody does it; nobody should

Show of hands: how many of you have been involved in, or know of, a school fundraising group that sets up accounts to credit the students and parents who participate in fundraising activities with the funds they raise? Common activity, right? The problem is that organizing any type of activity in which you keep track and credit only those people who sell the cookie dough or participate in the car wash with the money raised is not an allowable activity for a 501(c)(3) tax-exempt organization. Really? Really.

Helping students and their parents raise the money needed to travel to and march in the big city parade, or participate in gymnastics competitions, or other travel teams is common. How else will the students who can't write a $1,000 check participate? The problem is that these "cooperative fundraising" activities in which the members work together ("cooperate") to help each other pay off the high cost of participating in the sport, band, or other activity, are considered "private benefit" activities that are not allowed under IRS rules for 501(c)(3) charitable and educational groups.

IRS rules provide that nonprofit, 501(c)(3) groups must be operated ***exclusively*** to support their tax-exempt activities. None of their activities or funds may be used to help individual members raise money to pay personal expenses. This is a confusing concept that may be best explained with a little more background on why federal tax-exemption exist at all.

In the United States, all individuals, businesses and organizations that earn income are required to file and pay tax on their net earnings (aside from all the deductions, exceptions and complications that exist in the U.S. tax code). Certain organizations, however, are granted an exception to this rule, known as a tax-exemption. Tax-exemption essentially is a tax benefit that allows these groups to not pay federal income tax. In exchange for the tax-exemption, all of the activities of these groups must benefit the public in some way. None of their activities may be directed at helping specific individuals in the group (e.g. the people that participate in the fundraising).

I know what you're thinking: *How will you ever get anyone to fundraise if they don't get any benefit from helping out? How do you solve the "freeloader" problem?* Freeloaders are, in fact, the very essence of why groups are provided tax-exemption. For example, have you ever listened to public radio and not contributed to the fund drive? Is anyone barred from attending church if they don't throw money into the offering plate? Tax-exemption exists based on the idea that certain activities and services are needed in society as a whole, but everyone will not contribute equally to their continued existence.

Freeloader Solutions

There are, however, a few ways parent boosters may address the freeloader problem including:

1. set up a fair share donation program, and
2. conduct cooperative fundraising in a separate, taxable cooperative organization.

Fair Share Donation Programs

Fair share donation programs work by informing parents about the actual per-student cost of operating a specific school program and then asking parents to either donate their "fair share," or alternatively to volunteer to help raise the funds. The key to fair share donation programs is that contributions must be truly ***voluntary*** to be tax-deductible to the donor. Wording must be carefully drafted. Encourage but don't coerce donations. Here's an example:

ALL AMERICAN HIGH SCHOOL BAND BOOSTERS—ANNUAL FUND DRIVE

Dear Band Parents,

The All American High School budget contributes only a portion of the actual cost of operating the All American High School band. Your donations and help with fundraising events are essential to ensure that the band keeps marching in style.

This year the All American High School Band Boosters have been asked to raise $45,000 to supplement the school budget. With 150 students in the band this year, a contribution of $300/student is needed ($45,000/150 = $300).

Your support is vital. Please let us know how you are able to contribute your fair share to the band program this year.

I/We enclose a donation of $ ______________________ to support the band program

I/We agree to help with the following fundraising activities:

Car washes (October, December, March, May)

Candy bar sales (September)

Football game concessions

Other

Name of student: ______________________

Name of parent(s): ______________________

Email: ______________________

Email: ______________________

Cooperatives

If your group relies heavily on cooperative fundraising you might consider setting up a group that CAN legally undertake these activities. A cooperative is a type of legal entity that may operate for the individual benefit of the cooperative's members. Cooperatives may be established as nonprofit or for-profit organizations, or even as limited liability corporations. **Funds raised under a cooperative are taxable on the personal tax returns of the members who receive the income.**

IRS rules provide three key requirements for a cooperative:

1. voting in the cooperative must be democratic, with each member of the cooperative getting one vote;
2. all earnings of the cooperative must be distributed to the members in proportion to their time or other contributions to the cooperative; and,
3. IRS 1099-PATR must be issued to each member showing the earnings received each year by that member.

A school fundraising group may set up a separate cooperative fundraising entity each year and make it optional for the members of the group to join. Those who join may then elect the board and officers of the cooperative and participate in the cooperative's fundraising activities. The cooperative may track the hours each member volunteers, and/or the product sales of each member, and distribute earnings in accordance with each of the cooperative members' efforts within the cooperative.

I've been asked more than once how to handle a request from a parent who wants the money they raised to be returned to them by the school fundraising group when their child is no longer active in the group. I must tell them that the money raised in a 501(c)(3) organization can't be distributed to a member when they leave. Money raised by a member in a cooperative, however, may be distributed them when they leave.

The biggest downside of a cooperative? Some big money-making opportunities, such as volunteering to sell concessions at commercial sports venues, are only open to 501(c)(3) groups. This was a problem encountered by a fundraising group for a gymnastics competition team. They raised well over $20,000 per year by working concessions at a coliseum. The coliseum only worked with 501(c)(3) groups. The five families that did the majority of the volunteer work naturally wanted to be credited with "their earnings" from working the concessions. No matter how many different ways they proposed to distribute the money so that it was "fair," in the end all of the earnings raised by a 501(c)(3) group must be used for the good of the group as a whole and cannot be credited to those participating in fundraising.

A cooperative may, however, operate car washes, sell concessions at the school football games, sell candy bars and cookie dough, and other similar activities.

A link to the IRS publication, *General Survey of I.R.C. 501(C)(12) Cooperatives and Examination of Current Issues* is found on the More than Cookie Dough website **morecookiedough.com**.

10-SECOND TAKEAWAY

1. To determine the tax-deductible portion of a contribution made by a donor to a 501(c)(3) organization, the value of anything received in exchange for the donation must be deducted. The IRS has an exception, however, for small logo and other items with minimal value.
2. School fundraising groups recognized as 501(c)(3) charities by the IRS have more options to raise money, including applying for grants, and setting up "fair share" and other tax-deductible donation programs.
3. It's important to know and understand the IRS Qualified Sponsorship rules. Business sponsorship revenue is often classified as advertising income by the IRS; advertising income may be taxable to your organization, and may be deductible only as a business expense (and not a charitable donation) by the business sponsor.
4. Many states require groups to obtain a license prior to operating any type of game of chance (e.g. BINGO, or 50/50 raffles).
5. The funds raised by 501(c)(3) school fundraising groups must be used to support the group's mission; fundraising activities in which only the individuals who participate in the fundraising are credited with the funds raised are prohibited as private benefit activities.

9

Blending school staff and volunteers

School staff and volunteers don't always make the best sandwich cookie. Learn how to stick the two together for success.

Years ago when I was the president of the elementary school PTO we purchased an outdoor musical playground. I was excited about enhancing the playground equipment, and, as a mallet percussionist myself, I thought the outdoor xylophone was really cool! The musical playground was never installed by the school. The principal was concerned that the xylophone mallets might be used as weapons. A pencil could be used as a weapon I huffed. And what about the baseball that hit my daughter square in the head while she was in third grade? We thought she had a concussion!

I've learned a lot since then about the relationship between the school and the fundraising groups that support it, including that ultimately it is the school and not the parent volunteers that are liable for and decide about what equipment to install on the playground.

Being a school principal is a complicated job requiring the constant juggling of the diverse needs of the students, parents, teachers, administrators, school board, and the public at large. No matter how well-meaning we are as parent volunteers, sometimes tension arise between the volunteers and the school administration. How do we resolve this tension? How do we all just get along?

Understand the relationship

The first step is to understand the appropriate relationship between the booster club or other school fundraising group and the school. Each has an important, but different, role.

Generally speaking, the school and school principal and other staff are responsible for everything that happens on school grounds. If your group wants to meet in the school library, the school decides if you can. If your group wants to send flyers home with the students about the next fundraiser, you have to get the school's permission. If your group wants to hold a silent auction in the gym—you got it—the principal has yes/no authority over that one, too.

The fundraising group is responsible for managing it's operations, including obtaining and maintaining appropriate federal, state and local government registrations (e.g. 501(c)(3) status, state incorporation and fundraising registrations), organizing and operating its meetings, fundraising and other activities, and setting its budget and determining how to spend its earnings.

I like to think of the school fundraising group as grant-making organization that raises money to make grants to the school. The school is the grantee that approaches the school fundraising group and asks for grants for equipment and services not covered in the ordinary school budget.

Where schools and school principals, coaches, and other school staff advisory members of fundraising groups get into trouble is when they try to control too many aspects of the fundraising groups' operations, including how many fundraisers they may have, what types of fundraisers may be held and when, and how the funds of the group are spent.

For example, I recently spoke to volunteer of a football booster club in Florida that was surprised (shocked?) to find out that the football coach had contracted for football helmet reconditioning on behalf of the boosters without the boosters' knowledge. When the boosters got a bill for $10,000 that they couldn't pay, they called me for help.

There are several problems here. First, while schools are not required to offer non-academic extracurriculars like sports, if they do, the school should be responsible for covering the cost of all essential elements of the activity, including required uniforms and safety equipment. Second, the school—or in this case, the coach—should not, and generally cannot legally, contract with a vendor on behalf of the boosters.

On the flip side, booster clubs can get into trouble when they try to take on a role that should be left to the school. Booster clubs may weigh the fund requests brought to it by the school and decide what items the club is able, and willing, to fund. A booster club also may talk to the school about enhancements that boosters would like to make to the school, understanding, however, that ultimately the school decides what programs, activities, equipment, and supplies it provides to the students.

Boosters also should understand that once a gift is made to a school, the school can decide whether or not to use it as intended. Computers donated for the elementary school computer lab may be transferred to the middle school, if the school district decides that is what's needed. The elementary school principal was not required to install the outdoor xylophone our PTO purchased.

Communication is the key. Volunteers are more engaged if they feel that their interests are being heard. So, too, do school principals, administrators, and staff want to be heard. For those reasons, as well as matters of school liability, fundraising groups need to work closely with school administrators on any activities taking place on school grounds, or involving students, or the school, in any official capacity.

But what if your group is planning a silent auction off-site, perhaps in an empty store at the local mall. Can the school tell you whether or not wine may be served? This happened to me while serving as the elementary school PTO president.

We planned an off-site, adult-only silent auction. It was intended as a black-tie affair, complete with a complimentary glass of wine.

The principal balked, saying that alcohol should not be served at a school event. We argued that it was a PTO event that was being held off-site, for adults only. In the end, we agreed to forego the wine to keep the peace.

Let's say we had gone ahead, held the event, and served wine. What could the school have done? The principal could not have canceled the event. However, she could decide not to allow any communications about the event to be sent home in student back-pack mail. She also could decide not to accept any proceeds or grants from the funds raised at the event. In the end, we all have the same goal—enhancing student educational opportunities—and as a result cooperation between the school and the fundraising group that support it is essential to success.

When schools and booster clubs fail to establish clearly defined roles, confusion ensues. A case in point. I recently spoke to band parents about an annual trip for which they are raising money. In addition to raising funds, the band parents are providing volunteers to serve as chaperones. The band director asked the boosters to collect all student fees for the trip, determine the students that would receive a "scholarship" of all or part of the fees based on need, and send out and collect permission slips.

The band boosters contracted with a private bus company, and made hotel reservations. Students and their parents completed the standard school district permission slip for the trip. All chaperones were required to complete the school district's standard volunteer clearance form.

So is this a band booster trip or a school trip? The lines have been blurred.

The band is a school-sponsored activity. The band director is employed by the school, and handles the planning of the annual band trip. While band is a course for which students receive a grade, the annual band trip is an optional activity, similar to a field trip. The chaperones are school volunteers, cleared by the school. And the students complete school forms to go on the trip.

School or booster? I come down on the side of it being a school trip. The band boosters may raise money to cover all or part of the trip, recruit volunteers to serve as chaperones, and help the band director with trip logistics, including getting quotes or bids for transportation and hotels. Given that school forms need to be filled out for student participation and chaperone approval, however, it's a school trip, and the school, not the boosters, should contract for the transportation, hotels, and other needs of the trip.

Based on how much money the band boosters are able to grant to the school toward the trip, the school also should establish the student cost of the trip, and based on standard procedures (e.g. eligibility for the free or reduced cost lunch program) determine the students eligible for a full or partial waiver of the cost of the trip.

To recap, this table lays out the appropriate roles of fundraising groups and the schools that they support:

- Raises $$$$
- Obtains& maintains federal, state and local government registrations
- Determine operating rules (bylaws)
- Sets budget & fundraising goals
- Determines schedule of fundraising activities
- Recruits volunteers
- Provides input to school
- Votes on and makes grants to school for specific goods & services

- Advises group on the school needs & requests grant
- Receives grants
- Buys/contracts for goods & services
- Determines how school facilities are used
- Determine what communications may be sent home with students
- Determines when student fees are waived based on need

While I listed "determines schedule of fundraising activities" as a booster club role and responsibility, many schools ask that booster clubs submit their schedule of fundraising activities to the school for approval. This request by the school makes good sense in most cases. It helps the school ensure that multiple groups are not asking the community to buy cookie dough or wrapping paper at the same time, or that more than one silent auction is not being held simultaneously. The school also has to juggle the use of its facilities.

Note that I list "buys/contracts for good & services" under the schools' responsibilities. It is common for booster clubs to purchase equipment and other items and donate the equipment to the school. I don't recommend this, however. Seldom, if ever, does a grant-making foundation like the Ford Foundation or Kellogg Foundation buy equipment or other goods for the groups to which it makes grants. Instead, the grantee makes the purchases with the funds provided by the foundation. It is a good idea for schools and their support organizations to follow similar procedures. The booster club raises the money and makes a grant to the school for specific equipment, goods, services, etc. The school has the experience and procedures in place to purchase the needed supplies, equipment, or services. This places liability for whatever is purchased on the school. The school will be using and maintaining what is purchased, and has the greatest control over limiting any liabilities that arise from the purchase.

RECIPE FOR SUCCESS

School board rules regulating school fundraising groups are commonly found on the school districts' website. Look under "school board" and then "policies". These policies are often found under a section relating to community/home/parents and may be titled "community organizations" or relate to "parent involvement." You may also find policies relating to school fundraising groups under the budget and financial policies, including policies relating to accepting grants or donations from private sources.

SOMETHING TO CHEW ON

Use of the school name

Schools often have rules regulating the use of the school name (e.g. Central High School). To make sure that the booster club is distinguished as a separate activity from the high school, some schools ask that the booster club use the mascot in their name (e.g. Cougar Football Boosters versus Central High School Football Boosters).

I'm often asked whether this rule is enforceable. Generally government agencies, including public schools, cannot claim intellectual property rights (copyright, trademark) to their names and materials. In addition, common words (e.g. central, high school) are typically not eligible for trademark protection. Nevertheless, inappropriate use of a name could subject a group to fraud claims—e.g. if an organization claimed to be raising money for the Central High School Football team and instead used the money for children's cancer research. The school's rules are usually a good way to make sure that your group's name identifies itself and its activities

10-SECOND TAKEAWAY

1. Understanding the appropriate relationship between school staff and school fundraising groups is important for success.
2. Schools may control how school facilities and communication channels (e.g. backpack mail) are used.
3. School fundraising groups may control how they raise funds and how those funds are used to support the school.
4. Teamwork, however, is essential for success.

10

Adding in school fees

A few notes about boosters and school fees.

In the fall of 2015, Fairfax County Public Schools (FCPS), the 10th largest school district in the United States, announced that it expected to go from an $8 million budget shortfall during the 2015-2016 fiscal year, to a $100 million shortfall during the 2016-2017 fiscal year.

The district attributed the shortfall primarily to a growing student population, increases in state-required retirement contributions and increased health insurance costs. Because most of those costs were beyond the district's control, FCPS looked to increase student fees, and/or decrease programs to balance the budget. Among the items under consideration: reducing or eliminating sports and/or charging a participation fee of $150-200, and eliminating elementary school band and orchestra.

FCPS is not alone in its budget woes. The Center on Budget and Policy Priorities reports that at least 35 states are spending less per student now than they did before the 2007-09 recession. Pressure is on booster clubs to raise and contribute more toward the school budget, and on parents to pay more and higher fees for "non-academic" programs and activities.

The American Civil Liberties Union filed a lawsuit in 2010 against 35 public school districts in California, claiming that the schools' charges for art, home economics, music, sports, gym uniforms, and other classes and programs violated California's Constitution that requires that state to provide a free public education. The lawsuit was settled when the state adopted a new law (AP15750) requiring school administrators to be trained on how to raise additional funding without violating students' constitutional rights to a free education. The law also implemented a procedure for students and their parents to file complaints about illegal fees.

In 2013, the ACLU questioned a fee proposed by the Ann Arbor public schools for students who wanted to take an "optional" seventh period class. The ACLU argued that, because many students use the extra period during the school day to take courses required to graduate, the fee is illegal.

So what can schools charge for, and why do school volunteers need to know about this issue? When schools confuse the relationship between the school and their fundraising groups, the fundraising groups may be asked to collect fees from students that are in reality for school programs, and which may be against your state's free public education laws. In addition, charging and collecting fees may violate IRS rules that strictly prohibit school fundraising groups from having "work to fundraise, or pay a fee-or-don't-play" rules.

Here's a quick look at the current understanding of what types of fees schools may, and may not, charge:

Public schools may not charge fees for:	Public schools may charge fees for:
Tuition (unless a student is outside the district)	Non-graded, optional activities (e.g. dance, sports)
Graded courses, or activities that impact a grade	Food (subject to free & reduced-fee meals)
Cap & gown for graduation	Replacement costs (e.g. damage to school-owned books & supplies)
Necessary school supplies (drawing paper, pens, inks, blackboard erasers, crayons, lead pencils, composition books, bluebooks for exams, art material for art class)	Field trips & excursions (provided arrangements are made for students without sufficient funds)
	AP and other exam fees (provided taking the exam is not required or included as part of the course grade)
	Insurance made available by the school
	Parking fees

10-SECOND TAKEAWAY

1. Many states are spending less per student than they did before the 2007-2009 recession.
2. Pressure is on booster clubs to raise and contribute more toward school budgets.
3. Pressure is on parents to pay more and higher fees for non-academic programs and activities.
4. Some school fees may be found to violate free public education laws.

11

Don't get burned by Title IX

Why even boosters must be aware of the discrimination rules, and how fundraising can upset the balance.

Title IX, a federal anti-discrimination law, applies to groups that receive federal funds. So what does it have to do with booster clubs? A lot, as it turns out, especially for high school sports boosters. As you might imagine, allegations of discrimination are often emotionally charged, and it is easy for even the most well-intentioned boosters to get in a bind if you're not careful.

What's Title IX?

Any school that receives federal funds must comply with Title IX, a federal law that prohibits discrimination on the basis of gender. In 2011 alone, formal discrimination complaints were filed against 210 districts representing 525 high schools.

The most common complaints relate to unequal treatment for girls' and boys' athletic teams, including the equivalency of facilities, locker rooms, equipment, travel and transportation, coaching, and practice scheduling. Title IX does not require dollar-for-dollar matching. Rather, school districts must ensure that the overall opportunities for participation in sports are fairly equivalent for boys and girls.

School fundraising groups may upset the balance if, for example, the high school boys football boosters make a substantial donation that greatly enhances the boys' facilities as compared to the girls' facilities.

For example, in 2014, in response to the Department of Education's Office for Civil Rights (OCR) investigation of a Title IX complaint, the Plymouth/Canton, Michigan school district tore down bleachers that had been installed by the baseball booster club because it did not have the funds to otherwise equalize the boys and girls facilities.

The boosters spent six years raising the money for the bleachers so that they could change the configuration of the stadium seating and allow spectators a better view of the games, but similar facilities are not available at the adjacent women's softball field. The school system is holding onto the bleachers until it can find a way to meet the requirements of the OCR.

Although most Title IX complaints, to date, have been at the college and university level, experts say that greater enforcement at the K-12 level is on the horizon. It's more important than ever for schools to put in place practices and procedures for reviewing their Title IX compliance, and for booster groups to be aware of potential gender bias in their donations, to avoid wasted resources and hurt feelings.

RECIPE FOR SUCCESS

School districts can limit their Title IX liability by (1) encouraging coaches and athletic directors to stay involved with their booster clubs, including tracking fundraising goals and results for boys and girls sports; and (2) educating school booster clubs about Title IX and the requirements on schools to maintain substantially equivalent facilities for boys and girls sports.

10-SECOND TAKEAWAY

1. Title IX requires that schools ensure that overall opportunities for participation in activities, such as sports, are fairly equivalent for boys and girls.
2. Donations by school fundraising groups can tip the balance and cause facilities and opportunities to become unequal
3. Schools and fundraising groups must work together to determine how funds raised are used to avoid Title IX issues.

PART IV

The Icing on Top

12

Wouldn't You Rather Go Out to Eat?

Resources to let someone else do the mixing and baking, letting you enjoy the fruits of your labor more.

Operating a major industry like school fundraising with volunteer management and labor and very little training is crazy. Add almost continuous turnover, and you've got a recipe for trouble. At the same time, all evidence suggests that schools are becoming more, not less, dependent on donations from parent and community groups to supplements extracurriculars, and increasingly even core needs.

Fundraising efforts are especially important when it comes to leveling the playing field for kids of all economic circumstances to enjoy the enrichment and personal development such activities provide.

Given the high turnover within these organizations, principals and school business officers play an important role in ensuring that each year's class of well-meaning but often inexperienced volunteers are given the tools they need to run their organization like the business it is.

I founded Parent Booster USA (PBUSA) and wrote this book to help with that effort. Like it or not, there are lots of government regulations that apply to fundraising, with more risks and complexity being added each year. I want to make it easier for parent volunteers and the schools that they serve meet the growing fundraising rules and requirements.

The information, tools, and tips in this book, the appendices, and our companion website, **morecookiedough.com** are intended to do just that.

Still feeling overwhelmed? Parent Booster USA makes it easy! Here's how:

PBUSA offers assistance with obtaining federal tax identification numbers (EINs), incorporating with your state, and complying with state registration requirements.

PBUSA's Basic membership provides 501(c)(3) tax-exempt status under PBUSA's IRS group exemption. Our members do not have to complete Form 1023 or pay the IRS filing fees. Associate memberships are available for organizations that already have their own 501(c)(3) status.

Basic membership also provides tools, tips and information to operate your booster club, including sample documents & webinar training. And we are partnering with providers of document storage, bookkeeping software and other tools to make operating your school fundraising group easier than ever before!

Need even more help?

PBUSA's full service Get Legal membership includes help to incorporate your booster club, obtain a federal EIN for you, and register your organization with your state for sales tax exemption and fundraising.

Renew as a Stay Legal member and PBUSA will file your 990N* with the IRS, as well as the state reports and renewals required to keep your booster club in compliance in your state year after year. No more working hard to set everything up and have it all fall apart when next year's volunteers forget to make a filing.

Parent Booster USA is the only organization of its kind in the U.S. providing services to help school fundraising groups register as 501(c)(3) organizations and operate in full compliance with IRS, state, and local nonprofit regulations.

> *An additional, discounted fee applies for filing a 990EZ or Full 990. Contact PBUSA for further information.

Parent Booster USA makes problems go away for schools and the fundraising groups that support them. Our business goal is to be **THE one-stop shop** to keep school fundraising groups operating, pain-free, year-after-year.

Bonus materials including downloadable templates, links to other resources, and much more is available at the More than Cookie Dough companion website at: **morecookiedough.com**

Enter the reader password: **morecookiedoughplease!**

10-SECOND TAKEAWAY

1. Running an SSO doesn't have to be hard.
2. Parent Booster USA was created to ease your burden.
3. PBUSA is a one-stop shop for all your reporting/accounting/compliance needs.
4. PBUSA keeps the organizational history that often disappears when volunteers turnover.
5. 501(c)(3) status and a group exemption comes with PBUSA membership.

Appendices

Appendix A: All your 10-second takeaways in one place

1. School fundraising is big business. Treat it like one!
2. Volunteers are part-time, with little knowledge of the rules.
3. There is close to 100% turnover each year.
4. Not much is known about the parent-powered school fundraising industry, including how many groups exist, how much they are raising, and how the contributions of these groups impact the quality of education.
5. We know that most elementary schools in America have a parent teacher organization.
6. Most high schools have numerous fundraising groups, including athletic, music, academic, robotics, and many other booster clubs.
7. Most school fundraising groups are flying under the radar and are operating in violation of local, state and federal fundraising rules.
8. Incorporating your school fundraising group is highly recommended.
9. To organize properly in IRS lingo means that your formation document (e.g. articles of incorporation) includes all the required IRS language.

10. Make sure to obtain and use your group's own EIN, not the school's.
11. Obtaining 501(c)(3) status offers myriad benefits on both federal and state levels.
12. Federal tax returns must be filed annually, even if your group owes no taxes.
13. Your state has rules, too. Check and follow them!
14. School fundraising groups must be both *organized* and *operated* properly.
15. To be "operated properly" in IRS lingo means that all of your activities, including all the money raised, support your charitable and educational mission; none of your activities may be intended to help individual members of your group raise funds to help pay their personal fees or expenses of participating in the activity.
16. School fundraising groups should be run like a business, including keeping track of the money, and following IRS and state nonprofit fundraising rules.
17. Cloud-based tools for storing important records and documents make transitions of leadership easy.
18. All organizations that raise money—including nonprofits—must file an annual federal tax return.
19. Nonprofits seeking tax-exempt charity status must apply to the IRS for 501(c)(3) recognition or obtain 501(c)(3) status under an umbrella group like PBUSA.
20. If your group has failed to file tax returns, dissolve it and start over.

21. If you are faced with an IRS audit, know the rules and ask for help.
22. Incorporation happens at the state level and usually requires a fee and an annual corporate report identifying officers and contact information.
23. State taxes, including income, franchise and sales tax, are separate from federal tax and require separate applications for exemption.
24. Most states now require nonprofit groups to register prior to starting a fundraising campaign in the state.
25. Bylaws should reflect how you actually operate. Update them as needed.
26. School staff commonly should be advisory, non-voting members of school fundraising groups.
27. Preparing an annual budget, and implementing good financial practices and controls is essential.
28. Meetings should start and end on time, and provide an opportunity for input by those present. Meeting minutes should record only the actions taken and not details about the discussion.
29. Permission slips must be detailed and specific to allow parental consent that a court will uphold.
30. Most school insurance policies don't cover school fundraising groups. You need your own coverage.
31. To determine the tax-deductible portion of a contribution made by a donor to a 501(c)(3) organization, the value of anything received in exchange for the donation must be deducted. The

IRS has an exception, however, for small logo and other items with minimal value.

32. School fundraising groups recognized as 501(c)(3) charities by the IRS have more options to raise money, including applying for grants, and setting up "fair share" and other tax-deductible donation programs.
33. It's important to know and understand the IRS Qualified Sponsorship rules. Business sponsorship revenue is often classified as advertising income by the IRS; advertising income may be taxable to your organization, and may be deductible only as a business expense (and not a charitable donation) by the business sponsor.
34. Many states require groups to obtain a license prior to operating any type of game of change (e.g. BINGO, or 50/50 raffles).
35. The funds raised by 501(c)(3) school fundraising groups must be used to support the group's mission; fundraising activities in which only the individuals who participate in the fundraising are credited with the funds raised are prohibited as private benefit activities.
36. Understanding the appropriate relationship between school staff and school fundraising groups is important for success.
37. Schools may control how school facilities and communication channels (e.g. backpack mail) are used.
38. School fundraising groups may control how they raise funds and how those funds are used to support the school.
39. Teamwork, however, is essential for success.

40. Many states are spending less per student than they did before the 2007-2009 recession.
41. Pressure is on booster clubs to raise and contribute more toward school budgets.
42. Pressure is on parents to pay more and higher fees for non-academic programs and activities.
43. Some school fees may be found to violate free public education laws
44. Title IX requires that schools ensure that overall opportunities for participation in activities, such as sports, are fairly equivalent for boys and girls.
45. Donations by school fundraising groups can tip the balance and cause facilities and opportunities to become unequal
46. Schools and fundraising groups must work together to determine how funds raised are used to avoid Title IX issues.
47. Running an SSO doesn't have to be hard.
48. Parent Booster USA was created to ease your burden.
49. PBUSA is a one-stop shop for all your reporting/accounting/compliance needs.
50. PBUSA keeps the organizational history that often disappears when volunteers turnover.
51. 501(c)(3) status and a group exemption comes with PBUSA membership.

Appendix B: Governing document samples

B-1 Sample Articles of Incorporation

B-2 Sample bylaws

B-1 Sample Articles of Incorporation

TO: STATE CORPORATION COMMISSION:

The undersigned natural person of the age of twenty-one years or more, acting as incorporator, adopts the following Articles of Incorporation pursuant to Chapter 10 of Title 13.1 of the Code of Virginia as follows:

FIRST: The name of the corporation is **YOUR ORGANIZATION, INC.**

Insert the name of your organization

SECOND: The period of duration is perpetual.

This means the corporation continues indefinitely until dissolved.

THIRD: **The corporation is organized and will be operated exclusively for charitable and educational purposes within the meaning of 501(c)(3) of the Internal Revenue Code. (All references to sections in these Articles refer to the Internal Revenue Code of 1986 as amended or to comparable sections of subsequent internal revenue laws.)** Specifically, the corporation is organized to [INSERT BROAD MISSION STATEMENT].

In pursuance of these purposes it shall have the powers to carry on any business or other activity which may be lawfully conducted by a corporation organized under the Virginia Nonstock Corporations Act, whether or not related to the foregoing purposes, and **to do all**

things necessary, proper and consistent with maintaining tax exempt status under section 501(c)(3).

Bolded language is language required by the Internal Revenue Service (IRS) to qualify for 501(c)(3) tax-exempt status. In addition to the IRS language, insert a brief mission statement. It is a good idea to provide a broad mission statement in the articles.

FOURTH: The corporation may have one or more classes of members, the qualifications and rights, including voting rights, of which shall be designated in the bylaws.

Nonprofit corporations are not required to have members; however, most school fundraising organizations have members with voting rights.

FIFTH: The registered agent is **[INSERT NAME]** who is a resident of the state of Virginia and a director of the corporation, and the address of its initial registered office is **[INSERT STREET ADDRESS, CITY, STATE, ZIPCODE]** which is physically located in the County of **[INSERT COUNTY NAME]**.

States vary on who may serve as the registered agent. All states require that the person be a resident of the state with a street address in the state. Many states require the person to be a member of the corporation's board of directors or an officer. It is often a good idea for school fundraising groups to name a school staff person as the registered agent, as school staff typically turns over less frequently than school volunteers. The state must be notified, and a fee often must be paid, to change the registered agent. The registered agent is the person who receives all correspondence from the state, including any annual report that must be filed. The registered agent may need to be on the group's board of directors, but may be an officer that serves without vote. I recommend that school staff serve without voting rights.

SIXTH: The number of directors constituting the initial Board of Directors is **[NUMBER]**, and the name**(s)** and address**(es)**, including street number, of the persons who are to serve as the initial directors until the first annual meeting, or until their successors are elected and qualified, are:

[INSERT NAMES AND ADDRESSES OF INITIAL BOARD MEMBERS]

The members of the Board of Directors shall be those individuals elected, from time to time, in accordance with the Bylaws. Directors shall elect their successors.

States vary on the minimum number of board members required. Some states allow as few as one; many states require at least three. I recommend new boards consist of at least 3-5 members.

SEVENTH: **The internal affairs of the corporation shall be regulated by its Board of Directors as described in the Bylaws. Upon dissolution of the corporation, its assets shall be disposed of exclusively for the purposes of the corporation or distributed to such organizations organized and operated exclusively for charitable purposes which shall, at the time, qualify as exempt organizations under section 501(c)(3).**

Internal Revenue Service (IRS) required language to qualify under section 501(c)(3) of the Internal Revenue Code.

EIGHTH: No part of the net earnings of the corporation shall inure to the benefit of or be distributed to any director, employee or other individual, partnership, estate, trust or corporation having a personal or private interest in the corporation. Compensation for services actually rendered and reimbursement for expenses actually incurred in attending to the affairs of this corporation shall be limited to reasonable amounts. No substantial amount of the activities of the corporation shall be the carrying on of propaganda, or otherwise attempting to influence legislation and this corporation shall not intervene in (including the publishing or distributing of statements) any political campaign on behalf of or in opposition to any candidate for public office. Notwithstanding any other provision of these Articles or of any Bylaws adopted thereunder, this corporation shall not take any action not permitted by the laws which then apply to this corporation.

> Internal Revenue Service (IRS) required language to qualify under section 501(c)(3) of the Internal Revenue Code.

NINTH: The name and address, including street and number, of the incorporator is:

> The incorporator(s) simply serve as persons stating that they want this organization incorporated. Their duties end when the initial board meeting of the corporation is held. States vary in the number of incorporators required; typically from one to three incorporators.

B-2 Sample bylaws

[NAME OF BOOSTER ORGANIZATION]

Article I Name and Purpose

Section 1.01. Name. The name of this organization shall be [*NAME*].

Section 1.02. Purpose. The organization is organized and operated for the charitable and educational purposes of [*XXXX*] [*i.e., promoting competitive youth gymnastics; supporting XYZ High School, promoting music education, etc*].

Article II Membership

Section 2.01. Qualification. All parents, guardians or other persons with a child enrolled and attending [*SCHOOL*] and members of the licensed teaching staff shall be considered voting members of the organization. The Principal and Assistant Principals shall be non-voting, advisory members of the organization.

Section 2.02. Rights and Responsibilities. The members shall have the right and responsibility to attend meetings and events sponsored by the organization, serve on committees, and be nominated and elected to office. Voting members shall have the right to vote for the officers, review and approve the annual budget, and approve amendments to these bylaws.

Section 2.03. Quorum. The members present at any membership meeting of the organization, provided at least ten (10) members are present, shall constitute a quorum for the transaction of business. In the absence of a quorum the membership may not take action. In that event, any matter brought before the membership at a meeting at which a quorum is not present shall be discussed and decided by the Executive Board.

Section 2.04. Meetings. There shall be at least one general annual meeting of the membership in [*MONTH*]l at which the officers are elected. Such additional business or special meetings may be held alone or in conjunction with an event sponsored by the organization as is determined by the Executive Board or at the request of twenty (20) or more members in writing to the Executive Board.

Article III Executive Board

Section 3.01. Membership. The Executive Board shall consist of the elected officers of the organization.

Section 3.02. Authority. The affairs, activities and operation of the organization shall be managed by the Executive Board. The Executive Board shall transact necessary business during the intervals between the meetings of the membership and such other business as may be referred to it by the membership or these bylaws. It may create Standing and Special Committees, approve the plans and work of standing and special committees, prepare and submit a budget to the membership for approval, and, in general, conduct the business and activities of the organization.

Section 3.03. Meetings. The Executive Board shall meet monthly to prepare for general membership meetings and to conduct the affairs of the organization.

Section 3.04. Quorum. A quorum of the Executive Board for the conduct of business shall consist of at least three (3) officers in attendance.

Section 3.05. Action Without a Meeting. Any action required or permitted to be taken at a meeting of the Board of Directors (including amendment of these bylaws) or of any committee may be taken without a meeting if all the members of the Board or committee consent in writing to taking the action without a meeting and to approving the specific action. Such consents shall have the same force and effect as a unanimous vote of the Board or of the committee, as the case may be.

Section 3.06. Participation in Meeting by Conference Telephone. Members of the Board may participate in a meeting through use of conference telephone or similar communications equipment, so long as members participating in such meeting can hear one another.

Section 3.07. Reimbursement. Executive Board members shall serve without compensation with the exception that expenses incurred in the furtherance of the organization's business are allowed to be reimbursed with documentation in accordance with the organization's financial policies, and prior approval.

Article IV Officers and Their Elections

Section 4.01. Officers. The officers of this organization shall include one President, one or more Vice Presidents, a Secretary and a Treasurer and such additional officer(s) as may be elected or appointed by the Executive Board from time to time.

Section 4.02. Election. A nominating committee composed of the current President and at least one additional officer shall begin seeking nominees in [*MONTH*] of the year in which the candidates will be elected and develop a slate of candidates. The candidates shall be announced to the membership as soon as possible. Additional nominees may be solicited from the floor on the day of the election. Only those who have consented to serve shall be eligible for nomination, either by the committee or from the floor.

Officers shall be elected at the [*MONTH*] meeting of the organization by the members present. Officers shall assume their official duties on the last day of the current school year following their election.

Section 4.03. Term. Officers shall serve a one-year term. Officers may be elected for up to two consecutive terms in the same office.

Section 4.04. Vacancies. A vacancy occurring in any office shall be filled for the unexpired term by a person elected by a majority vote of the remaining members of the Executive Board.

Article V Duties of Officers

Section 5.01. President. The President shall be the principal executive officer of the organization and, subject to the control of the Executive Board shall in general supervise and control all of the activities of the organization. The President shall be a member of the Executive Board and, when present, shall preside at all meetings of the Executive Board and all meetings of the membership. The President shall vote only in the case of a tie in a vote of the Executive Board or the membership. The President shall select and appoint the chairpersons of all Standing and Special Committees and shall be an ex-officio member of all committees of the organization.

Section 5.02. Vice-President(s). The Vice-President shall be a member of the Executive Board and, in the absence of the President, shall perform the duties of the President. The Vice-President shall perform such other duties as are assigned by the President or the Executive Board.

Section 5.03. Secretary. The Secretary shall be a member of the Executive Board. The Secretary shall keep the minutes of the proceedings of the membership and the Executive Board, shall see that all notices are duly given in accordance with these Bylaws, shall be responsible for the publishing of meeting minutes, shall manage and keep an accurate tally of the volunteer records and, in general, perform all duties incident to the office of Secretary and such other duties as may be assigned by the President or the Executive Board.

Section 5.04. Treasurer. The Treasurer shall be a member of the Executive Board. The Treasurer is the authorized custodian to have oversight of all funds of the organization in accordance with the organization's financial policies. The Treasurer will organize, document, and record all financial activities. The Treasurer will be diligent and conscientious in ensuring all funds are received and spent in accordance with the organization's tax-exempt purpose, bylaws and budget. The financial records belong to the organization and must be available to the other officers and members upon request.

The Treasurer shall:

- Prepare an annual budget for review and approval by the members.
- Ensure that numbered receipts are provided for cash received by the organization.
- Ensure that all funds are timely deposited in the organization's authorized bank account(s).
- Ensure that payments and disbursements are authorized by approved budget, or an amendment to the budget.
- Present a written financial report (including income and expenditures and comparing budgeted amounts to actual year-to-date amounts), at each General Membership Meeting of the membership and at other times as requested by the Executive Board.
- See that an annual financial review or audit, as appropriate based on budget size, is conducted and presented to the Executive Board, General Membership, and other stakeholders.
- Maintain financial records (including financial reports, checkbook, bank statements, deposit slips, cash tally sheets, documentation regarding transactions, IRS Form 990 documents, etc.) and turn all over to the new treasurer.

Article VI Finances

Section 6.01. Budget. The Executive Board shall present to the membership at the first regular meeting of the membership after the officers have been elected, or as soon thereafter as practicable, a budget of anticipated revenue and expenses for the year. This budget shall be used to guide the activities of the organization during the year, including serving as approval for anticipated expenditures.

Any substantial deviation from the budget must be approved in advance by the membership.

Section 6.02. Obligations. The Executive Board may authorize any officer or officers to enter into contracts or agreements for the purchase of materials or services on behalf of the organization.

Section 6.03. Loans. No loans shall be made by the organization to its officers or members.

Section 6.04. Checks. All checks, drafts, or other orders for the payment of money on behalf of the organization shall be signed by the Treasurer or by any other person as authorized in writing by the Executive Board, except that checks of $250 or more must have the signature of at least two officers, such as the Treasurer and the President. Checks shall bear notice of this requirement above the signature line as follows, ***"Two signatures required for checks in the amount of $250 or more."***

Section 6.05. Banking. The Treasurer shall ensure that all funds of the organization are timely deposited to the credit of the organization in such banks or other depositories as determined by the Executive Board. All deposits and disbursements shall be documented by a receipt, an invoice, or other written documentation. Sequentially numbered receipts shall be provided, with a copy kept, whenever cash is turned over or collected. All deposits and/or disbursements shall be made as soon as practicable upon receipt of the funds, normally daily, immediately after received and counted.

If debit or credit cards are established in the name of the organization, a policy approved by the Executive Board shall be developed and used that includes a list of the authorized users, daily/

monthly/annual spending limits, and review and oversight provisions. No personal charging on the card by the authorized users shall be allowed.

Section 6.06. Financial Controls. The organization shall adopt appropriate financial controls to ensure the integrity of its funds. Specifically, without limitation, the organization shall maintain separation of financial controls so that, minimally:

- All expenses must be approved by the membership by way of approval of an annual budget, or amendments thereto, or be approved by separate resolution of the Executive Board;
- Two people must be present to count cash. Cash should be counted on-site where it's collected. A cash tally sheet, signed by both counters, must be used to record the totals. Cash should then be deposited immediately into the bank account.
- Checks exceeding $250 must be endorsed by at least two officers authorized by resolution of the Executive Board, and checks of the corporation shall include above the signature line a notice to this requirement;
- An officer or other person without check signing authority designated by the Executive Board shall review and reconcile all bank statements on a monthly basis; and,
- A committee of at least two (2) persons without check signing authority shall annually audit all corporate finances, or hire and supervise an outside accountant or auditing firm to conduct a review of corporate financial records.

Section 6.07. Financial Report. The Treasurer shall present a financial report at each membership meeting of the organization and prepare a final report at the close of the year in accordance with the organization's financial policies. The Executive Board shall have the report and the accounts examined annually. If the organization grosses less than $100,000 per year, the financial practices and accounts may be reviewed by an internal audit committee. The audit committee shall consist of two or more Board or voting members of the organization who are not involved in the routine handling of the organization's finances, including not having signature authority on bank accounts or approval authority over disbursements. If the organization grosses over $100,000 in receipts, an external professional, such as a certified public accountant (CPA), shall be hired by the audit committee to perform a financial review or compilation. A full audit shall be conducted by an external CPA when annual gross receipts equal or exceed $250,000.

Section 6.08. Fiscal Year. The fiscal year of the organization shall be from June 1 to May 31, but may be changed by resolution of the Executive Board.

Section 6.09. Financial Record Retention. All records of the organization shall be maintained and destroyed in accordance with law, and standard record retention guidelines. Financial records shall be maintained as follows:

RECORD	HOW TO STORE	PERIOD OF TIME
Year-end Treasurer's financial report/ statement, annual Internal Financial Review Reports, IRS Form 990s	Store in corporate record book, binder, or cloud-based software.	**At least seven (7) years** Consider keeping permanently.
Bank statements, canceled checks, check registers, invoices, receipts, cash tally sheets, investment statements, and related documents	Compile & file records on a yearly basis. Store in binder or cloud-based software.	**Seven (7) Years** Store w/financial records. Destroy after seven years.
Treasurer's reports (monthly)	Compile & file records on yearly basis. Store in binder or cloud-based software.	**Three (3) Years** Store w/ financial records. Destroy after three years.

Article VII Conflicts of Interest

Section 7.01. Existence of Conflict, Disclosure. Directors, officers, employees and contractors of Corporation should refrain from any actions or activities that impair, or appear to impair, their objectivity in the performance of their duties on behalf of the Corporation. A conflict of interest may exist when the direct, personal, financial or other interest(s) of any director, officer, staff member or contractor competes or appears to compete with the interests of the Corporation. If any such conflict of interest arises, the interested person shall call it to the attention of the Board of Directors for resolution. If the conflict relates to a matter requiring board action, such person shall not vote on the matter. When there is a doubt as to whether any conflict of interest exists, the matter shall be resolved by a vote of the Board of Directors, excluding the person who is the subject of the possible conflict.

Section 7.02. Nonparticipation in Vote. The person having a conflict shall not participate in the final deliberation or decision regarding the matter under consideration and shall retire from the room in which the Board is meeting.

However, the person may be permitted to provide the Board with any and all relevant information.

Section 7.03. Minutes of Meeting. The minutes of the meeting of the Board shall reflect that the conflict was disclosed and the interested person was not present during the final discussion or vote and did not vote on the matter.

Section 7.04. Annual Review. A copy of this conflict of interest statement shall be furnished to each director or officer, employee and/or contractor who is presently serving the Corporation, or who hereafter becomes associated with the Corporation. This policy shall be reviewed annually for information and guidance of directors and officers, staff members and contractors, and new officers and directors, staff members and contractors shall be advised of the policy upon undertaking the duties of their offices.

Article VIII Indemnification

Every member of the Executive Board, officer, or employee of the Corporation may be indemnified by the Corporation against all expenses and liabilities, including counsel fees, reasonably incurred or imposed upon such members of the Board, officer or employee in connection with any threatened, pending, or completed action, suit or proceeding to which she/he may become involved by reason of her/his being or having been a member of the Board, officer, or employee of the Corporation, or any settlement thereof, unless adjudged therein to be liable for negligence or misconduct in the performance of her/his duties. Provided, however, that in the event of a settlement the indemnification herein shall apply only when the Board approves such settlement and reimbursement as being in the best interest of the Corporation. The foregoing right of indemnification shall be in addition to, and not exclusive of, all other rights which such member of the Board, officer, or employee is entitled.

Article IX Amendments

These Bylaws may be amended at any regular or special meeting of the membership by a majority vote of the members present, provided that at least thirty (30) days' notice of the proposed amendments has been made to the membership, or alternatively the membership waives the required notice.

Appendix C: IRS registrations and documents

C-1 About IRS Form SS-4 Application for EIN

C-2 IRS Form 1023EZ

C-3 IRS Form 1023

C-4 Changing your booster club's year end

C-1 About IRS Form SS-4 Application for EIN (employer identification number)

An employer identification number (EIN)—sometimes called a taxpayer identification number (TIN)—is the corporate equivalent of a Social Security number. It is issued by the IRS and identifies your organization for tax purposes. Every business or other organization must have an EIN to open a bank account, file a tax-exemption application, or file a tax return.

School fundraising groups are legally separate from their schools and must obtain their own EINs. Anytime a new school fundraising group is incorporated, a new legal entity is created that must then obtain a new EIN to distinguish itself from any prior organization, and to identify the organization as a new group to the IRS.

EINs are available, at no charge, through the IRS' online application system at: **https://sa.www4.irs.gov/modiein/individual/index.jsp**

Or you can simply search "EIN online" and look for the official IRS website.

To apply for an EIN you will need:

- the legal name of your organization
- the organization's address
- an officer or director's name, phone number, and Social Security Number.

The IRS EIN system asks a series of questions about your organization. Some of the questions may be confusing. For example, school fundraising organizatons normally check the "other tax-exempt organization" instead of the "corporation" box where it asks for corporate structure. Note also that the EIN system does not accept any punctuation, including, for example, a period after "Inc."

The EIN system is open Monday-Friday, 7:00 a.m. to 10:00 p.m. Eastern Standard Time.

Upon completion of the online application you may ask for your IRS EIN letter "CP575" online for immediate download. **Keep your CP575 letter in your permanent records. The IRS does not issue replacements.**

What an EIN is not

The EIN does not identify a business as for-profit or nonprofit, taxable or tax-exempt. An EIN is simply the number that identifies your organization to the IRS. You can, however, use an organization's EIN to look up its tax status in the IRS database of tax-exempt organizations.

An organization's EIN also is sometimes mistaken as providing proof of state income or state sales tax-exemption. Again this is not the case. State income tax, sales tax exemption and fundraising registration are all handled by your state.

When to get a new EIN

If you dissolve a prior organization, such as an unincorporated fundraising group, and create a new organization, such as an incorporated school fundraising group, you must get a new EIN for the new organization. This distinguishes the old group from the new group. It's a good idea to distinguish the name of the new group from the old group as much as possible, including adding "Inc." to the incorporated entity's name and also changing other words in the name. For example, the All American High School Boosters may become the All American HS Warrior Boosters, Inc. Otherwise you run the risk of the IRS merging the old entity with the new entity, and getting the IRS to unmerge the groups can be a nightmare.

Close out an old EIN account

To close out an old EIN account, you may send a letter to the IRS asking that the business account associated with the old EIN be closed at:

Internal Revenue Service
ATTN: EO Entity
Mail Stop 6273
Ogden, UT 84201
Or fax to: 801-620-7116

C-2 Form 1023EZ

Smaller organizations that expect annual gross income during each of the first three years to be less than $50,000 may apply for IRS 501(c)(3) tax exemption using the online Form 1023EZ. The first step in the process is to go to the pay.gov website and register for an account. Then you search for, and complete the IRS Form 1023EZ.

To determine if your group is eligible to use the online short-form application, be sure to review the Form 1023EZ eligibility worksheet found in the instructions for Form 1023EZ at: **http://www.irs.gov/pub/irs-pdf/i1023ez.pdf.**

C-3 Form 1023

Form 1023 is a longer, paper form. You can download a copy from the IRS website at: **http://www.irs.gov/pub/irs-pdf/f1023i.pdf**

C-4 Changing Your Booster Club's Year End

Nonprofit 501(c)(3) organizations must file their annual IRS information return, Form 990-series, not later than the 15th day of the 5th month after the close of their fiscal year. Failure to file, on time, for three consecutive years means loss of tax-exempt status.

The return due date is based on the IRS' record of your organization's fiscal year end date. As a result, you should check the IRS records to make sure you know the date the IRS has on record, and if your group is following a different fiscal year, make sure you let the IRS know.

You can either mail the change to the IRS, or fax it in. Both a sample letter and mailing address, and fax and fax number, are included here for your reference.

REGULAR MAIL

To: Internal Revenue Service
1973 North Rulon White Boulevard
Attn: EO Entity
MS 6273
Ogden, UT 84201

From: <CLUB NAME>
<CLUB EIN>
<GROUP EXEMPTION NUMBER 5271>
<DIRECTOR NAME>
<ADDRESS FOR CLUB>
<CONTACT PHONE NUMBER>

Date: <DATE>

Dear IRS Service Agent:

I write with regard to ______ <YOUR BOOSTER CLUB's NAME>______, ______<YOUR BOOSTER CLUB's EIN> ______. We request that you change our Club's tax year end to ______<NEW MONTH>______, effective immediately.

Foranyquestionsregardingthistaxyearchange,pleasecontactmeat (___) ____ – __________.

Thank you for your prompt attention to this matter.

Sincerely,

______<YOUR NAME>______, ______<BOARD POSITION>______

I recommend that you when you mail anything to the IRS you send it certified, return receipt. Keep a copy of your letter, and the return receipt notice in your records.

FACSIMILE

To:	IRS EO Entity	**From:**
Fax:	(801) 620-6236	**Pages:**
Phone:	(801) 620-6019	**Date:**
Re:	Change of Tax Year End	

▶ *Urgent* ▶ *Action* ☐ *Please Comment*
☐ *Please Reply* ☐ *As Requested*

This fax is in regard to________________ <YOUR BOOSTER CLUB's NAME>________________, ________<YOUR BOOSTER CLUB's EIN> ________. We request that you change our Club's tax year end to ________<NEW MONTH>________, effective immediately.

Please acknowledge receipt by calling (___) ____—__________.

Thank you for your prompt attention to this matter.

Sincerely,

____<YOUR NAME>______, ____<BOARD POSITION>______

Appendix D: Operation guidelines

D-1 Recruiting, Training, and Retaining Volunteers.

D-2 Tips and Strategies to Run Great Meetings

D-3 ParliPro Basics for Conducting a Meeting

D-4 All about meeting minutes

D-5 Sample meeting minutes

D-6 Sample permission slip

D-7 Officer transition guidelines

D-1 Recruiting, Training, and Retaining Volunteers

Volunteers can be invaluable in assisting with fundraising and providing extra helping hands for school staff. Here's a few tips on how to obtain, train, and retain volunteers.

Recruiting Volunteers

1. Recruit widely. Don't limit your request for volunteers to your usual circle of friends, but reach broadly into the school and community. For example, my church provides volunteers to the nearby school, and my elementary school PTO received help from the local Coast Guard facility for our labor-intensive fall festival. Some community members simply want to help make their community a better place.
2. Recruit more volunteers than you think you'll need. Remember, many hands make light work, and no-shows and dropouts are inevitable.
3. Seek out volunteers at the beginning of the year, providing a form with many options. Also include how much time each volunteer opportunity takes. You will get more volunteers if they understand the time commitment and don't feel like they are jumping into a black hole of unending obligations.
4. Provide as much detail as you can about the volunteer roles and what you hope to accomplish. Descriptions, photos, and outcomes from prior years will help engage your prospective volunteers. Testimonials from prior volunteers who enjoyed working with your group also may help.

5. Don't stop at one appeal. Many times prospective volunteers are busy when first asked but may be more receptive if you ask again at another time. This also shows that you are not a closed group, but encourage wider participation.
6. Ask people personally for their help. Don't rely entirely on an email notice or written appeal. Go beyond passive messaging by reaching out personally to potential volunteers and ask your other officers and volunteers to do the same. Some people respond better if they are asked personally.
7. Make an appeal for volunteers prior to each new event. This lets people who have a connection or interest in the type of event to get involved.
8. Sometimes local businesses will provide staff to nonprofits as volunteers. It doesn't hurt to ask!
9. Sometimes people like to contribute what they know how to do best, their special or unique skills. A painter may contribute a painting. A baker might donate a cake. However, other people prefer a break from their day jobs. Keep an open mind, and encourage people to volunteer where they feel best.
10. Check with your school and, if required, make sure volunteers complete all required school information forms and background checks.
11. Make sure you have at least two people present when interacting with students or children; you also should have two people onsite when counting cash and signing checks.
12. Don't forget to get the students involved!

Training Volunteers

1. Provide volunteers with any training and/or tools needed to do their jobs properly. Don't assume a volunteer understands what to do and how to do it. However, also encourage volunteers to offer suggestions for improving how things are done.
2. Group training can be a time saver; however, make sure you consider the normal work schedules of your volunteers. You may need to do both a work-hour, and an evening, training.
3. Make sure your trainers are good with volunteers. Working with a volunteer work force requires more collaboration than an employer/employee relationship.
4. Develop and keep written records of your programs, processes, and procedures. Having a guidebook for the annual fall festival that lists all the vendors previously used, the number of volunteers needed, and so forth makes it easier for next year's volunteers to continue your good work. Consider keeping your written notes and guidelines in cloud-based online storage for ease of transferring your knowledge to next years volunteers. It sure beats the shoebox or notebook approach.
5. Holding a "launch" meeting for a new project or fundraiser helps get everyone on the same page regarding expectations and responsibilities, and helps everyone get excited about the new challenge.
6. If a volunteer is struggling with an assignment, consider sending in reinforcements and finding the volunteer an assignment that is a better match.
7. Competitions and inexpensive incentives help recruit and retain volunteers and keep them excited about the work along the way.

Retaining Volunteers

1. To keep people happily working without pay, you need to understand what motivates them, and keeps them fulfilled.
2. It helps if you make volunteering for your group convenient and fun. Offering opportunities to socialize and make connections between volunteers, school staff and students also is a good motivator. Volunteers also want to know that they are appreciated.
3. Flexibility with respect to volunteer tasks, hours, and the way things get done is helpful.
4. Balance difficult tasks with fun ones.
5. Some volunteers stay motivated if they feel like they have special privileges or perks. These are perks that cost the group nothing (i.e. a special parking place for the volunteer of the month), but go a long way to say thank you.
6. Give praise and kudos to volunteers in your newsletter and other communications.
7. But remember, while some folks like awards, praise and thanks, others may prefer to be anonymous. Make sure you ask!
8. Make sure your volunteers have something to do. When I went to help at the church food pantry, and there were so many volunteers I had nothing to do, I was less motivated to go back. I felt like they didn't need me.

D-2 Tips and Strategies to Run Great Meetings

It's not easy to lead a meeting and successfully encourage participation and different points of view. Establishing an agenda that includes standard financial and other reports made at each meeting is the first step to a well-run meeting. While using basic parliamentary procedure is a good idea, I recommend that you steer clear of trying to enforce Roberts Rules of Order. The few people who understand Robert's Rules may use the complicated procedures to control a meeting, rather than to encourage participation by all. Here are a few tips to help you lead effective meetings:

Prepare a detailed agenda in advance

- Give each agenda item a specific amount of time, to help ensure that the meeting runs according to plan and no one person or topic overruns the entire meeting.
- Place topics that may require more discussion at the beginning of the agenda.
- Use action verbs on each agenda item (i.e., decide, share, review, select, discuss, finish, adjust, etc.) to ensure a clear outcome.

Start on time / end on time

- Schedule time to socialize 15 minutes before meeting begins, or encourage socializing after the meeting ends.
- Start on time. End on time. It shows that you respect everyone's time.
- Set a timer or stopwatch to go off at the time the meeting is to begin, as a signal for all to be quiet.

- Designate a timekeeper to watch the clock during the meeting, and give feedback to meeting participants to let them know when the time for discussion on an agenda item is almost up, to keep the meeting on track.

Stay on topic

- Have the meeting Chair (i.e., Booster Club President) stop the "runaway" discussions and return to the agenda item being discussed.
- Create a "Parking Lot" on a piece of paper, where important issues not related to current discussion can be listed, to be discussed at a later date.
- Use the "Parking Lot" when creating the next month's agenda.

D-3 Parlipro Basics for Conducting a Meeting

Simplified parliamentary rules are a good choice when it comes to running effective school fundraising group meetings. Having no rules for meetings leads to unorganized, often chaotic meetings, while using a strict Roberts Rules of Order method may lead to imbalanced meetings, dominated by those few who understand Roberts Rules. Following these simple rules ensures that all voices are heard and hopefully better decisions are made.

1. Chair calls the meeting to order.
2. Meeting participants review agenda. Amendments, if any, are proposed to the agenda. Participants approve agenda.
3. Once the agenda has been approved, including the time period to begin and end discussion of each item, the agenda may not be changed or amended without a motion to amend the agenda, a second, and approval by a 2/3 majority affirmative vote.
4. The Chair conducts the meeting, allowing the indicated time period for discussion and/or presentation of each item.

Six Steps to Every Motion

1. A member is recognized and makes a motion.
2. Another member seconds the motion.
3. Without rewording, the presiding officer restates the motion to the assembly.
4. The members debate the motion. No member may speak for a second time until all members who wish to speak are heard once.
5. The presiding officer asks for affirmative votes & then negative votes.
6. The presiding officer announces the results of the vote.

D-4 What to Include (and leave out) of Meeting Minutes

Minutes serve as the official record of the actions that occurred at a meeting. While there is often a desire to make minutes as complete as possible so that they serve as a historical record, including too much detail may be unwise from a legal perspective.

Minutes should include four basic types of information:

1. time, date and place of the meeting;
2. the fact that proper, prior notice was given or that such notice was waived by those attending the meeting;
3. the names of those in attendance and whether a quorum was present; and
4. the official actions taken by the meeting participants (motions made and approved or defeated).

Not required to be included in minutes are:

1. names of those who move and second motions;
2. the vote (number voting for and against) for each motion;
3. detail of the debate that occurred regarding each motion.

Minutes may be looked at if your group is ever investigated or sued. Therefore, it is important to keep an accurate record of your meetings but not include unnecessary information that could prove harmful in the future. Including the names of those who move and second motions can help potential plaintiffs find "friends" and "foes." Providing vote counts in the minutes makes public how divided the assembly was, and are unnecessary. Only the fact that a motion passed or failed is needed. Unless a meeting participant specifically requests that their negative (but not prevailing) vote be recorded, you can leave it out of the minutes. Because debates infrequently reflect a balanced view or consensus of the members (either the minority or majority view may be more strongly argued) inclusion of debates in the minutes may create a skewed historical record. In addition, including debate detail may create a public appearance of divisiveness when a united public front may be more desirable.

The minutes should include the date, time and place of the meeting, along with a list of who attended, whether a quorum was present, and that proper notice of the meeting was given (or waived). To make the minutes easier to draft and use, it is a good idea to have the minutes follow the agenda. For each item on the agenda, there should be a corresponding item in the minutes. In this way, the supporting reports and documents may be attached to, and kept as part of, the agenda. Someone reviewing the minutes may then easily reference the agenda and attachments.

Keeping minutes simple by recording only the actions approved, but not the detailed debate, balances the need for a complete record against the risks of including too much information.

D-5 Sample Meeting Minutes

NOTE: Report on actions taken. It is not recommended to report on discu ssions and the actual vote count, unless unanimous. Minutes are a public record.

[BOOSTER CLUB NAME]
[DATE]
[LOCATION]

Proper written notification of this meeting was provided to board members XX days in advance of the meeting. The following board members were present: [NAME, NAME, NAME].

1. **Call to Order**
   The meeting was called to order at [TIME] by [NAME].

2. **Approval of Minutes**
   [NAME] moved to approve the minutes of the last board meeting held on [DATE]. Motion was seconded and the minutes were approved.

3. **Financial Policies**
   Financial policies for the organization were discussed. The following policies were approved: The President and Treasurer shall have check signing authority. To ensure proper financial controls, the Vice President (who does not have check signing authority) shall review monthly bank statements.

4. **Programs**

   The next event of [DESCRIPTION] was discussed. [NAME] reported that donations have been secured to cover all costs of the event.

5. **Other Business**

   No other business was discussed.

6. **Next Meeting**

   The next board meeting shall be held on [DATE], [TIME] at [LOCATION].

7. **Adjourn**

   The meeting was adjourned at [TIME].

D-6 Sample Permission Slip

Courts are reluctant to uphold permission slips that are written broadly with a parent giving up the right to sue for injury to their child. Courts often find that the parent did not really have enough information or details about the risks to sign away their legal rights. A permission slip can never stop a lawsuit claiming damages, and there is no certainty how any particular judge will look at a permission slip. However, the template below provides guidance on drafting an "informed consent" document with a better chance of providing your group or school protection from liability.

[INSERT NAME OF SPONSOR OF THE EVENT]

IN CONSIDERATION of the right of

[**INSERT STUDENT NAME**] who is called "Student" in this agreement, to attend and participate in [**INSERT NAME OF ACTIVITY**], which is called "Activity" in this agreement, the parent/guardian of the above-identified Student:

1. Understands and agrees that [NAME OF SPONSOR] is the Sponsor of this Activity;
2. authorizes and gives the Student permission to participate in the Activity;
3. understands that the Activity will include:

[INSERT DETAILED DESCRIPTION OF THE ACTIVITY INCLUDING

1. THE METHOD OF TRANSPORTATION
2. THE ACTIVITIES THE STUDENT WILL ENGAGE IN
3. WHERE the ACTIVITIES WILL BE HELD (E.G. INDOORS, OUTDOORS) risks
4. IF FOOD WILL BE SERVED AND IF SO WHAT TYPE OF FOOD, WHO IS PREPARING the food
5. And any and all other relevant details]

4. consents to have the Student [initial one box]

   ☐ participate in all portions of this Activity

   ☐ participate in all portions of this Activity, except:

   [provides an opportunity for the parent to opt-out of having their student participate in some of the activities]

5. acknowledges that there is an element of risk involved in any activity involving,

[INSERT DETAILED LIST POTENTIAL RISKS]

6. certifies that the Student is physically, mentally, and emotionally capable of attending and participating in the activities
7. assumes all risk of and financial responsibility for any loss or injury to the Student or others that may occur as a result of the Student's negligence or misconduct

8. indemnifies and holds the SPONSOR harmless from and against any and all costs, claims, demands, charges, liabilities, obligations, judgments, executions, costs of suit and actual attorneys' fees incurred or suffered by SPONSOR as a result of, or arising out of, the Student's negligence or misconduct;
9. authorizes SPONSOR to obtain or authorize any reasonable incidental and/or emergency medical treatment for the Student in the event the Student's parent(s)/guardian(s) are not readily located and Student becomes ill, injured or incapacitated; and,
10. accepts responsibility to pay for any medical or other treatment provided to the Student while on the Activity.

The parent(s)/guardian(s) signing below on behalf of STUDENT acknowledge that they have read this consent and understand its contents and voluntarily consent to its terms.

____

Printed Name of parent/guardian

____

Signature of parent/guardian

Date: __________________________

Cell phone #: ______________________

NOTES: Note that in item #3 and again in #5 should be as specific as possible regarding the activities involved, and the related risk. The idea is that parents cannot provide consent unless they understand the nature of the activity and the real risks. In item #7 and again in #8 the consent form refers to the parent and student being responsible for claims or injuries that arise from the student's "negligence or misconduct". The form does not ask the parents and students to be responsible for "any and all claims" or other language that often is considered overbroad by courts. The rationale is that the school or sponsoring organization should be liable for its own negligence or oversight, while the student and parents are responsible only for their negligence or oversight.

D-7 Transitions

Booster Board and Officer Transition Recommendations

It is important that your organization's permanent records and financial documents be handed over to the new incoming officers. Transitions are easier if you store all your documents in Internet cloud-based storage, and use online bookkeeping software to keep your financial records. PBUSA provides cloud-document storage for its members, and partners with several bookkeeping vendors to provide online financial software.

Your booster club's permanent records should include:

Permanent records

Articles of incorporation (if your group is incorporated as a nonprofit in your state)

Bylaws (including documentation of prior amendments)

IRS EIN letter (Form CP575)

Verification of 501(c)(3) status (e.g., IRS determination letter or PBUSA membership certificate)

State income tax exemption documents (if any)

State sales tax exemption documents (if any)

State fundraising registration documents (if any)

Year-end financial report and statement

Financial records

IRS 990-series return (990N, 990EZ or full 990)—three (3) most recent returns must be publicly available upon request

Report from your annual internal financial review

Treasurer's reports either quarterly or monthly

Financial documents

Bank statements and bank reconciliation reports

Cancelled checks

Check registers

Invoices and receipts

Cash tally sheets

Investment statements (if any)

Other helpful documents

Calendar / Timeline

Budget / Spreadsheets / Statements

Publicity (fliers, posters, emails, etc.)

Vendors used (w/ helpful info such as "recommended" or "do not use")

Feedback / Suggestions for improvement

Ideas for next year

Appendix E: Financial procedure guidelines & templates

E-1 Financial policy worksheet

E-2 Sample budget worksheet

E-3 Sample financial policies

E-4 Sample cash tally box receipt

E-5 Step-by-step guidelines to conduct an internal financial review

E-6 Surviving an IRS Audit

E-7 Cloud accounting software

E-1 Financial policy outline

1. Approve an annual budget

A. Include expected sources of income & amounts

B. Include expected types of expenses & amounts

C. Review periodically budget versus actual income/expenses

2. Implement financial controls

A. Require 2 signers on every check

B. Have all expenditures approved by someone other than check signer

C. Have bank statements reviewed/reconciled by someone other than check signer

D. Always use 2 people to count cash on site at each fundraiser/event; record receipts on cash tally sheet; deposit funds immediately to bank

3. Keep good records

A. Receipts for all expenditures

B. Deposit slips

C. Cash tally sheets

D. Bank statements

E. Federal (IRS Form 990) and state tax returns/fundraising reports

4. **Use bookkeeping software**
   (allows you to keep receipts and important documents all in one place for easy reference)

5. **Conduct an annual financial review**
   A. Use a committee of at least 2 people who were not routinely responsible for money handling
   B. Follow guidelines for what to look at and for, such as PBUSA's *Guide to Conducting an Internal Financial Review*
   C. Consider allowing the school business or other officer to review the booster club's books

E-2 Sample budget worksheet

	BUDGET	ACTUAL
INCOME		
Fundraiser 1		
Fundraiser 2		
Fundraiser 3		
Individual donations		
Business sponsorships		
TOTAL INCOME		
EXPENSES		
Fundraiser 1 costs		
Fundraiser 2 costs		
Fundraiser 3 costs		
Business sponsorship costs		
Grants to school		
TOTAL EXPENSES		
Net (carry-over to next year)		

E-3 Sample financial policies

Financial Controls for the [NAME OF SCHOOL FUNDRAISING GROUP]

Annual Budget. An annual budget that shows expected sources of income and line items showing the amount expected from each source, and expected expenses and line items showing the amount of each expected expense, shall be developed by the Executive Committee shortly after their election, and presented to the membership for review and approval. The annual budget may be amended from time to time by the membership, as needed.

Purchase Approval. All purchases on behalf of the organization must be pre-approved, either by detailed line item in the annual budget or vote of the board or membership. The officer(s) authorized to sign contracts on behalf of the organization shall be designated in the bylaws, or by vote of the Board of Directors or membership.

Bank Account(s)

1. **Bank accounts.** All bank accounts of the organization shall be opened in an FDIC insured institution, approved by the Board of Directors, in the legal name of the organization using the organization's own EIN (employer identification number). Bank accounts shall not use the school's EIN.
2. **Investments.** All investments and investment accounts shall be approved by the Board of Directors. Investment accounts shall generally be limited to Certificates of Deposit in FDIC insured institutions.

3. **Bill payment.** All bills of the organization shall be paid by check from the organization's bank account. Online or e-checks are permissible, however all procedures for paper checks be followed, regardless of the banks procedures (prior approval of processing the online payment should be obtained by way, for example, of email approval by the required number of signatories before processing the payment).

   A. All checks shall be numbered and shall be held in the custody of an officer authorized by the Board, such as the Treasurer.

   B. All payments by check shall correlate to an invoice or receipt, on which the check number and date paid shall be written. If a receipt or invoice is not available, an officer shall write and sign a description of what was purchased.

   C. Pre-signing blank checks is prohibited.

   D. Two signatures are required on any check of $250 or more. The requirement for two checks should be printed on the checks above the signature line as follows, "Two signatures required for amounts of $250 or more."

   E. All expenses must be pre-authorized by (i) approval in the annual budget, or (ii) subsequent amendment to the budget, or (iii) vote of the Executive Board if authorized by the bylaws.

   F. Bank statements shall be reviewed by the treasurer and one or more other officers without signature authority to ensure separation of financial controls.

4. **Bank cards.** If debit/credit cards are established in the name of the organization, a policy approved by the Executive Board shall be established that includes a list of the authorized users,

daily/monthly/annual spending limits, and limits use to charges for the organization. No personal charging on the card by the authorized users shall be allowed.

Cash

1. All cash must be kept in a secure location, such as in a lock box. A cash box ledger shall be kept and monthly cash box reports, including starting balance, expenditures, additions, and ending balance shall be provided to the Board.
2. The Executive Board shall establish a maximum amount of cash kept on hand, such as $250.
3. A receipt shall be provided whenever cash is turned over or collected.
    A. Receipts shall be numbered and kept in a bound book, with one copy provided to the person turning in the cash, and one copy kept in the receipt book as a record. Alternatively, a receipt ledger on which the date, amount, and signature of both the giver and recipient of the funds may be used.
    B. Cash should always be counted by two (2) individuals, on the day the funds are collected, and at the site (i.e. school) where the funds are collected. A cash tally sheet showing the date and amount collected, and signed by the counters, should be maintained. If the Treasurer is not one of the counters, the Treasurer should re-count the funds, and counter-sign the tally sheet,
    C. Cash should be deposited immediately into the organization's bank account. A copy of the deposit slip shall be immediately forwarded and kept by the Treasurer. The deposit slip should

be cross-referenced against the cash tally sheet, and saved for the bank reconciliation.

Financial Reports. The Treasurer should provide a financial report to the officers, and members as appropriate, usually monthly that includes:

1. Statement of receipts and disbursements (also known as a Statement of Activities);
2. Balance sheet (includes cash on hand, other assets, liabilities and equities);
3. A copy of the bank statement, bank reconciliation, monthly cash reports and imaged checks;
4. A copy of the cash tally sheets; and,
5. Any outstanding receipts/expenses/purchase orders/contractual obligations.

The monthly treasurer's reports shall be compiled and kept in the organization's records for three (3) years. Bank statements, canceled checks, check registers, invoices, receipts, cash tally sheets, investment statements, and related documents should be kept for seven (7) years. The year-end treasurer's report, annual financial review report, and IRS Form 990 shall be kept permanently.

E-4 Sample cash tally sheet

Cash Box Tally Sheet

Beginning Cash Box

Date: ____________

Function: ____________

Cash Box ____________

Coin:

______	X $0.01	= $______
______	X $0.05	= $______
______	X $0.10	= $______
______	X $0.25	= $______
______	X $0.50	= $______
Total Coins		______

Currency:

______	X $1	= $______
______	X $5	= $______
______	X $10	= $______
______	X $20	= $______
______	X $50	= $______
______	X $100	= $______
Total Currency		______

Beg. Cash Box Total ______

Signatures

Rec'd by: ____________

Rec'd by: ____________

Rec'd by: ____________

Event Proceeds

Date: ____________

Function: ____________

Cash Box: ____________

Coin:

______	X $0.01	= $______
______	X $0.05	= $______
______	X $0.10	= $______
______	X $0.25	= $______
______	X $0.50	= $______
Total Coins		______

Currency:

______	X $1	= $______
______	X $5	= $______
______	X $10	= $______
______	X $20	= $______
______	X $50	= $______
______	X $100	= $______
Total Currency		______

Checks ______

Total Cash & Checks ______

***Less Beg. Cash Box** ______

Net Proceeds ______

____
Signature

____
Signature

____
Signature

*This amount remains in cash box until event competed.

E-5 Conducting an internal annual financial review

An annual financial review of the organization's records should be completed at the end of the year, and prior to turning records over to new officers. The financial review may be completed by an internal audit committee, if the organization has gross receipts of less than $250,000 per year. Below are step-by-step guidelines to help your financial review committee complete the review. Remember, this review should be conducted by 2 or more volunteers without signature authority on the bank account(s) and who were not regularly involved with the day-to-day financial operations of your organization. This review provides a new set of eyes on the books.

Step #1: Gather financial documents including:

- ☐ Copies of all written financial policies
- ☐ Copies of treasurer's reports for the year (or other period) to be reviewed
- ☐ List of all bank and investment accounts, including names of persons authorized to sign on each account
- ☐ Copies of all bank and other financial statements for the period to be reviewed
- ☐ Copies of all bank and investment account reconciliations for the period to be reviewed
- ☐ Cash tally sheets or Cash receipts journal
- ☐ Invoices, receipts, and other documents
- ☐ Documentation of any restrictions on the use of any particular funds or donor gifts

- ☐ IRS letter documents, including most recent Form 990, IRS letter recognizing tax-exempt status, and IRS letter assigning an EIN (employer identification number) to the organization.

Step #2: Review financial documents and processes.

- Check the organization's EIN (employer identification number) as assigned by the IRS against the EIN used on the organization's bank and other financial accounts. Make sure the school's EIN is not being used.
- Check names of persons authorized to (a) approve transactions and (b) sign checks, against:
  - persons authorized to conduct these activities in the organization's minutes; and,
  - bank records indicating who is authorized as a signatory.
- Check to ensure that the person(s) who sign checks are not the same, or only, person(s) reviewing monthly bank statements.
- Check all bank reconciliations to determine that the beginning balance of one month is the same as the ending balance of the previous month. Also note whether the balance listed on financial statements is the same as the balance listed on the treasurer's reports presented to the organization.
- Pick one month and perform a bank reconciliation using the original records. If you find a discrepancy between your reconciliation and the reconciliation provided by the person who performed the original reconciliation, research the discrepancy to find the error or explanation for the discrepancy.

- Count all cash in petty cash accounts to ensure that the count agrees with the books.
- Check to see if the organization carries fidelity bond coverage on people handling the organization's funds; if insurance is not held, propose that the organization consider obtaining bonding coverage.

Step #3: Review income and receipts.

Determine if the deposits listed on the financial reports provided to the organization match deposits listed on bank statements. Check to see if cash tally sheets match the amount of cash reported as received from an event on financial reports, and also match the deposit indicated on bank statements.

Step #4: Review disbursements.

- Test to be sure that payments made were properly authorized—by a line item in the approved budget, an approved amendment to the budget, or an appropriate vote authorizing the expenditure.
- Test purchase orders to be sure that they were properly approved and match the actual disbursement or invoice.
- Review records to ensure that there is an invoice, receipt, or other appropriate written documentation for each disbursement, and that the amounts match.

Step #5: Review tax/information returns.

Review financial records to ensure that appropriate federal (IRS Form 990) and state income tax/information returns have been timely filed.

Step #6: Review financial control systems.

- Check to evaluate whether financial duties have been appropriately separated. Although it can be difficult for small organizations to separate financial duties, certain separations are essential for appropriate financial controls. These separations protect both the organization, and the individuals handling the finances. Specifically:
  - Individuals with signature authority should NEVER approve the transactions/disbursements for which they sign. All expenditures should be approved in an annual budget, as originally approved or amended, or by a vote of the board or membership as appropriate. All disbursements should be documented by an invoice, receipt or other appropriate written documentation.
  - The individual(s) with signature authority may reconcile bank statements. However, at least one additional officer or director should review monthly bank statements, or bank statements may be included with the treasurer's report to the board/membership.
  - Finances should be reviewed annually by an audit committee that consists of two or more individuals who do not routinely handle the organization's finances, such as by being a signatory on the accounts.

  - Cash should always be counted by at least 2 persons at/near the time received, and then recounted by the treasurer or other individual prior to deposit.

Step #7: Review reporting systems to ensure adequate information is provided for the organization and its officers/directors to make reasonable decisions.

- Are reports from the treasurer timely and complete?
- Are financial policies, including separation of financial controls, being followed?
- Are all records being gathered (invoices, receipts, cash records, checks and disbursement records, bank records, treasurer's reports) so that they can be reviewed as needed, and only discarded in accordance with the organization's record retention guidelines?

Step #8: Write a report.

The financial review/audit report should document at a minimum:

- Steps taken in the financial review
- Current fund(s) balance and balance sheet
- Comments, if any, on any concerns or discrepancies found and the audit committee's recommendations to correct these concerns or discrepancies.

E-6 IRS audit worksheet

Following are the key do's and don'ts with respect to each of the 5 nonprofit organization areas of compliance that the IRS often audits.

1. Private benefit–the rule

Officers/directors/key employees receiving inappropriate financial benefit—unreasonable salaries/benefits

Do

- ✔ Document board approval of salaries
- ✔ Document comparability data used
- ✔ Document details of any transactions between the organization and officers/directors/key employees and/or their for-profit businesses

Don't

- ✔ Approve your own (or a family members') salary
- ✔ Approve excessive benefits
- ✔ Approve transactions that provide excess value to officers/directors/employees

2. Commercial activities–the rule

Nonprofit organizations may not compete with for-profit entities

Do

- ✔ Know & document how your organization's activities differ from a commercial/for-profit entity
- ✔ Price your services at or below fair market value; document
- ✔ Know if your services are "for the convenience" of your members; document
- ✔ Know & document how any joint ventures with for-profit companies benefit the nonprofit; make sure that the board of directors approves the transaction; ensure that the transaction does not provide excess benefit to the for-profit

Don't

- ✔ Engage in the same or similar activities as for-profits
- ✔ Charge the same fees for the same activities of for-profits
- ✔ Undertake a contract with a board member at a fee higher than you may obtain the same services from another source

3. Change in activities–the rule

IRS rules provide that you must notify the IRS of any significant change(s) in your organization's activities.

- by written notice
- on next filed 990-series return

Do

✔ Have the board approve any change in your activities

✔ Notify the IRS of the change

✔ Document the foregoing in the minutes and organization records

Don't

✔ Make changes that require a new exemption application

✔ Make changes without board approval/documentation/IRS notice

4. Lobbying and political activities–the rules

- 501(c)(3)s may engage in an "insubstantial amount" of lobbying, but may not engage in any political activities.
- Lobbying requires a request for action (draft bill, vote yes/no) on a specific piece of legislation.
- Political activity is assisting someone to run for office.

Do

✔ Make the 501(h) election if your organization does any substantial lobbying

✔ Track all lobbying expenditures

✔ Set up a separate 501(c)(4) or political action committee if you plan to engage in lobbying and/or political campaign activity

5. Board of directors–the rule

Nonprofit organizations must have an independent board of directors.

Do

✔ Document officer/director elections in the minutes

✔ Document board actions in the minutes

✔ Keep minutes concise—record actions only

Don't

✔ Include only family/related members on board

✔ Compensate board members as board members

Recommended Documentation Tips:

Keeping the following records is good business practice, and will help ensure you are ready if the IRS ever makes a house call.

Board minutes

- Record actions and no-vote counts
- Record evidence of arms-length transactions (joint ventures)
- Record comparability data examined (salaries)
- 990 review
- Conflict of interest policy
- Whistleblower policy

Contracts with board/officers/key employees

- Record arms-length steps
- Reviewed/signed by disinterested persons
- Comparability data

Financial records

Provide only what is requested

Consider paper versus electronic

Adopt policies for what you keep/destroy; document in writing

- *IRS 990-returns* 7 years
- *Year-end financial report* Permanent
- *Periodic financial reports* 3 years
- *Bank statements & related* 7 years

Review and understand **IRS rules and procedures**:

- Know the IRS rules
- Request a delay
  - Request time whenever needed
  - IRS must complete audit within three years of the tax return in question
- Don't agree to host the audit at your office (field audit)
  - Ask that the audit be conducted at the IRS office
  - Field audits, on average, result in higher adjustments
- Don't agree to repetitive audits
  - IRS may not examine the same issue(s) if an IRS audit of either of the two preceding years resulted in a no-change

It is essential to **review IRS Publications**:

- IRS publications
  - Compliance Guide for 501(c)(3) Public Charities
  - A Day in the Life of an Exempt Organization Audit
  - The Examination Process, Audits by Mail (Publication 3498-A)
  - The Examination Process (Publication 3498)
  - Your Rights as a Taxpayer (Publication 1)
  - How to Appeal an IRS Decision on Tax-Exempt Status (Publication 892)
  - IRS Web Pages
  - **http://www.irs.gov/Businesses/Small-Businesses-&-Self-Employed/IRS-Audits**
  - **http://www.irs.gov/Individuals/Forms-and-Publications-About-Your-Appeal-Rights**

E-7 Cloud-based accounting and recording keeping software

Using cloud-based software is a tremendous help to school fundraising groups and other organizations where volunteer turnover is high. No more changing recordkeeping methods or software each year. Pass on the password and the financial records are moved instantly to next year's treasurer, along with the all the organization's financial history. And using financial software makes creating reports, and distributing them, much easier.

Appendix F: Fundraising tools

F-1 Quick Reference Guide to Fundraising

F-2 Best practices for running a fundraiser

F-3 Sample donation request letter

F-4 Sample cash/in-kind donation form

F-5 Sample donor receipt

F-1 Quick Reference Guide to Fundraising

1. **Funds must support a <u>public</u> tax-exempt purpose**
   - For example—amateur athletics, K-12 education, or performing arts
   - Funds must support an entire team (or competition team); not just individuals who helped raise money
   - May not purchase equipment (provide assets to) a for-profit school

2. **Cooperative fundraising/IFAs (individual fundraising accounts) are not tax-exempt activities**
   - Includes ANY activity to raise money and then credit the individuals that raised the money or helped with the fundraising to pay the personal costs of the activity for those participating in the fundraising; typically those who do not help with the fundraising must pay their full costs or not participate in the activity
   - Because these activities benefit only the fundraising participants and not the broader public tax- exempt purpose of the organization, these activities are personal benefit activities rather than tax-exempt activities
   - Tax-exempt organizations must engage exclusively in tax-exempt activities; any significant amount of personal benefit activities bar exemption

3. **Know & advise donors what is tax-deductible**
    - Voluntary payments to 501(c)(3)s for which the donor receives nothing of value in exchange for the donation/payment are fully tax-deductible
    - The value of anything substantial (think more than a lapel pin, newsletter or mug) must be subtracted from the payment to determine the tax-deductible portion
    - The 501(c)(3) is responsible for telling the donor the deductible portion

4. **"Fair share" donations**
    - Voluntary payment of amount suggested by an organization as the cost per student to participant in an activity
    - Payments must be voluntary (strongly encouraged, but not required for participation; language used must be clear that payment is voluntary)

5. **Raffles, Bingo and other "games of chance" have special rules**
    - Many states, counties and/or cities require you to register before undertaking games of chance
    - In many places, games of chance are not legal
    - It's important to check your state and local rules

6. **Sales tax**
    - Some states provide exemption, upon application, for items purchased by 501(c)(3) orgs for use by the group

- Some states require registration, collection and payment of sales tax on items sold by your group to raise funds
- It's important to check your state and local rules

F-2 Best Practices for Running a Fundraiser

1. **Ensure proper financial controls are in place before the fundraiser begins**

   Finances / Financial Controls

   - Ensure all funds raised are used for the tax-exempt purpose of the organization.
   - Approve a budget of anticipated revenue and expenses for the year (to include each fundraiser).
   - Authorize a club officer(s) to enter into contracts or agreements for the purchase of materials or services for the fundraiser on behalf of the organization (authorization usually given through an Executive Board).
   - Update signature cards for the booster club bank accounts with names of those who have check-signing authority.
   - Accept only check or e-payment donations rather than cash to avoid theft
   - When collecting cash at a fundraising, always have two unrelated people present to collect and count the cash.
   - Ensure two people sign all checks.
   - Designate two people, one without check signing authority, to review all bank statements.

- Avoid making loans from the organization to any officers or members.

Treasurer

Appoint a Treasurer who is responsible for all funds of the organization in accordance with the organization's financial policies, including but not limited to, the following:

- Receives all funds and gives receipts for monies due and payable to the organization from all sources.
- Deposits such funds in a bank or other organization as selected by the Executive Board, as soon as practicable upon receipt of the funds.
- Signs checks, makes disbursements as authorized by the budget, as approved, or amended, by the membership.
- Presents a financial report at each membership meeting detailing all financial transactions related to the fundraising event.

2. **Promote your 501(c)(3) status to potential donors/buyers:**
   - Provide evidence of your 501(c)(3) status to donors (e.g. IRS determination letter or your PBUSA membership certificate)
   - Ask potential donors to send their donations to an address or mailbox specifically designated for use by the booster club; don't have donations sent to a member's home.

3. **Don't use Individual Fundraising Accounts (IFAs)**

   IRS rules prohibit 501(c)(3) organizations from undertaking fundraising activities in which only the students or parents who participate are given "credit" for the money raised.

F-3 Sample donation request letter

Date

Potential Donor Name
Company
Street Address
City, State, Zip

Dear ________________,

The **[NAME OF ORGANIZATION]** is proud to support our students and honor the hard work they do. We invite you to support your local community by making a donation. We depend on the generosity of the surrounding community to provide the best opportunities for our children in light of drastic cuts to education budgets.

Only with your help can we continue to provide the level of support our students need and deserve. All donations are tax-deductible to the extent allowed by law. **[NAME OF ORGANIZATION]** is exempt from federal taxes under section 501(c)(3) of the Internal Revenue Code.

Thank you for considering a donation to this very worthy cause. For questions or further information, please contact

________________________.

Sincerely,

[NAME OF CONTACT PERSON]
[NAME OF ORGANIZATION]

Please send gift certificates, monetary donations, and correspondence to:

[NAME AND ADDRESS OF CONTACT PERSON]
[NAME OF ORGANIZATION] EIN#: **[XX-XXXXXXX]**

F-4 Sample cash/in-kind donation form

Yes! We want to help the **[NAME OF ORGANIZATION]**. The **[NAME OF ORGANIZATION]** is tax-exempt under section 501(c)(3). All donations are tax-deductible.

Date: ______________________________

Cash Donation: $ ____________________

In-Kind Donation: Please describe your donation (including deductible value):

____

____

[An in-kind donation is deductible to the extent of your cost, and not fair market value, if it is being sold by our organization at an auction or other event, or used as a prize. Only items used by our organization to further our mission (other than for fundraising purposes) are deductible at full fair market value.]

Please PRINT clearly and list your name(s) as you would like to be recognized on our [WEBSITE, PROGRAM, HANDOUT, ETC.]:

Company/Organization Name:

Contact Name(s): ______________________________

Phone: ______________ Email: ______________

Address: ______________________________

Contact information is needed to send a tax receipt for donations. If you do not receive a response from us within 30 days, please e-mail **[CONTACT PERSON WITHIN YOUR ORGANIZATION]** so we can verify that your donation has been received.

Please mail this form to:

[NAME AND ADDRESS OF CONTACT PERSON]

Thank you for your support!

[NAME OF ORGANIZATION]
[ADDRESS]
[CITY, STATE, ZIP]
[EIN #]

F-5 Sample donor receipt

[NAME OF ORGANIZATION]

Date

Donor Name
Company
Street Address
City, State, Zip

Dear ______________________,

Thank you for supporting **[NAME OF ORGANIZATION]**. Your generosity is greatly appreciated and will go a long way to support the (band, football team, etc.).

[Select and insert only the one paragraph that applies]

OPTION 1 (fully deductible contribution)
We appreciate your donation of $ ____________. The **[NAME OF ORGANIZATION]** is recognized by the Internal Revenue Service as a 501(c)(3) organization. As a result, your donation is fully tax-deductible to the extent provided by law and based on your tax situation. No goods or services were received in exchange for your donation.

OPTION 2 (partially deductible contribution)
We appreciate your donation of $ ______________. We are happy to provide you with annual VIP seats to all home football games in appreciation for your contribution. The value of this gift is $100. The **[NAME OF ORGANIZATION]** is recognized by the Internal Revenue Service as a 501(c)(3) organization. As a a result, the amount of your donation, less the value of the gift ($100), is tax-deductible to the extent provided by law and based on your tax situation.

OPTION 3 (in-kind contribution)
We appreciate your donation of [INSERT DESCRIPTION OF IN-KIND ITEM, E.G. hand-held vacuum cleaner] for our upcoming silent auction. The **[NAME OF ORGANIZATION]** is recognized by the Internal Revenue Service as a 501(c)(3) organization. IRS rules provide that in-kind donations that are sold by a tax-exempt organization at a fundraiser are tax-deductible to the extent of your cost basis in the item. Items are tax-deductible at full fair market value only if the item is used by the tax-exempt organization to further its mission and activities in a way other than to raise funds.

Thank you again for your donation.

Sincerely,

[NAME OF CONTACT PERSON]
[CONTACT INFORMATION]

Appendix G:
Parent Booster USA Model School District Policy

This model policy was developed by Parent Booster USA, Inc. (PBUSA) to assist schools, school districts and their respective administrators to understand best practices for working with school fundraising groups.

Schools in this school district must maintain clear roles distinct from the roles of the organizations that provide support to the schools. Each school must manage its own activities in accordance with school policy and state law, including without limitation collecting student fees for classes and school-conducted extracurricular activities and contracting for and purchasing items to be owned and used by the school. School fundraising groups act as grant-making organizations responding to requests from schools/school staff for support needed (volunteers and funds) that is not provided in the ordinary operating budget. At no time, however, should school fundraising groups act as an agent of the school to collect student fees for classes and other school activities, determine or provide waivers of such fees, or engage in other activities as an agent of the school.

Schools within this school district may cooperate with, including providing use of school facilities for meetings and activities, and accept funds from school fundraising groups (i.e. parent-teacher-student organizations, sports, arts, academic and other booster clubs) provided the school fundraising group meets the following requirements:

1. **Organize as a nonprofit corporation** including:
   A. Filing incorporation documents in the state and maintaining such corporation in good/active standing with the state by filing state-required annual or other reports;
   B. Adopting and abiding by a set of bylaws that outlines the organization's operating procedures;
   C. Electing officers in accordance with the procedures set forth in the bylaws; providing the names and contact information of the officers to the principal of the school that the organization primarily supports; updating the principal when the officers change.

2. **File all required state registrations**, including state fundraising registration requirements.
3. **Obtain and identify the organization using its own federal tax identification number** (also known as an employer identification number or EIN); school fundraising groups may not use the school's EIN.
4. **Be recognized by the Internal Revenue Service as a 501(c)(3) organization**, and maintain such status by annually filing the required IRS 990-series return.

5. **Adopt and abide by appropriate financial controls.**
6. **Provide monthly financial reports.** Provide periodic (usually monthly) financial reports to the organization's officers and members that include at least a statement of receipts and disbursements, a copy of the bank statement(s), and a copy of the cash tally sheets.
7. **Conduct annual financial review/audit.** Appoint an audit commit consisting of officers/members who are not signatories on the bank account to conduct a year-end financial review of the organization's records. Provide the review to the new officers of the organization with a copy to the principal or other designated administrator of the school the organization primarily supports. The Better Business Bureau Standards for Charity Accountability (available at **www.give.org**) provide that the annual financial review may be completed by an internal audit committee provided the organization's gross receipts do not exceed $250,000/year. Larger organizations should hire an outside financial professional, such as a certified public accountant, to complete the financial review.

CPSIA information can be obtained
at www.ICGtesting.com
Printed in the USA
BVHW04s1337120418
513079BV00032B/967/P